PAGES FROM STAGES

Anthony Field

**ENTERTAINMENT
TECHNOLOGY PRESS**

Reference Series

PAGES FROM STAGES

Anthony Field

Entertainment Technology Press

Pages From Stages

© Anthony Field
Editorial ©Paul Webb

This edition published July 2004 by
Entertainment Technology Press Ltd
The Studio, High Green, Great Shelford, Cambridge CB2 5EG
Internet: www.etnow.com

ISBN 1 904031 26 9
A title within the
Entertainment Technology Press Reference Series
Series editor: John Offord

CODE / PFS004-04-05

CONTENTS

ACKNOWLEDGEMENTS 9

INTRODUCTION II

1 THEATRE ROLES 17
Becoming a Playwright 17
Playwriting: How the System Works 21
Script for Success.. 25
Becoming An Angel 27
Theatre Management – an Introduction 29
Theatre Management 32
Television Stars and the Theatre 34

2 PERFORMING ARTS SCHOOLS 37
It's Got to be All or Nothing – The School for
    Performing Arts.. 37
Chairman Sets His Sites on Fame 41

3 THEATRE CATERING 43
An Introduction... 43
Introduction to Theatre Catering 46
Theatre Catering 48

4 THEATRE PROMOTION 51
Introduction to Ticket Prices 51
Directing a New Course 51
Ticket Prices – Seat Price Shuffle 54
Theatre Size – an Introduction 57
Theatre size... 59
Small But Perfect... 61
How to Broaden the Appeal of the Arts
    – an Introduction 63
How to Broaden the Appeal of the Arts I 65

How to Broaden the Appeal of the Arts 2 70
Tourism and Theatre – an Introduction 72
Tourism and Theatre 74

5   AUDIENCE REACTION 79
Audience Reaction 82
To Boo or Not to Boo 84

6   THEATRE ISSUES 87
Theatre – A Millenium Survey – an Introduction 87
Theatre – A Millenium Survey 89
Has Broadway More Buzz – an Introduction 93
Has Broadway More Buzz 95
What's the Future of the RSC 98
ISPAA – What's it All About? 100
Reacting to Revolution 100
Getting in on the Act 105
Regions at Risk 108
A Helping Hand 110
Rights and Wrongs – Intellectual Property Rights 112
Precious Preservation 115
On the Wrong Track 119

7   MUSICALS 121
Are Musicals More Fun – an Introduction 121
Are Musical More Fun 123
Producing a Musical 127
Matching Musicals to Theatres 131
The Economics of The Orchestra 135

8   THE ARTS COUNCIL 143
The Arts Council - an Overview 143
Arts Council and Creativity – Use Your Imagination 144
Subsidy and the Commercial Theatre 147
Building Jerusalem 150
Politicians and the Pot of Gold 152
The Pot of Gold at the End of a Subsidised Rainbow 154

9 LECTURES 159
    Commitment and Responsibility Recalled 159
    Commitment and Responsibility 160
    Assets and Achievement – an Introduction 172
    Assets and Achievement 173

POSTSCRIPT 181

INDEX 187

ACKNOWLEDGEMENTS

Apart from my great debt of gratitude to Paul Webb for his assiduous work as editor of this book, I also recognise the enormous assistance and advice I have received over the past half a century of my professional life from my colleagues at the Arts Council of Great Britain and Theatre Projects Consultants Limited, particularly its Chairman and great lighting designer, Richard Pilbrow.

I have also benefited from the unstinted support as well as friendship from:

Kelvin J. Allen
Nicholas Allott
Robert Breckman
Barry Burnett
John Dankworth
John Elsom
Paul Farrah
Mark Featherstone-Witty
Thelma Holt
Dame Cleo Laine
Peter Longman
Alistair MacKay
Sir Cameron Mackintosh

David Pelham
John Pick
Mike Power
Richard Pulford
Claire Rayner
Rupert Rhymes
Douglas Schwalbe
Kenny Wax
Duncan Weldon
Jean White
Peter Wilson
and many others

This is not to mention my three wonderful secretaries over all these years: Brenda Jordan, Norma Davies and Elizabeth Lomas who has borne most of the day-to-day work on this book and is thankfully still with me.

Special gratitude is due to John Causebrook who has diligently proof-read these pages and compiled the index.

Finally, this book is dedicated to my one and only Ted. When we dined with Elaine Stritch I introduced Ted to her as my 'better half', she responded by saying: "I am so glad you didn't call him your partner as I always think then of Marge and Gower Champion and Astaire and Rogers. As you are not dancing partners, you might call him your one and only!" – and he has been for over fifty years.

Anthony Field

INTRODUCTION

As I pick up my pen – yes, I still write in longhand and my colleagues on their computers smile indulgently at my quill pen – I have a very real sense of déjà vu since I have written a number of introductions to books which have never reached publication. In 1977 Professor John Pick, then at the City University, wrote to me 'I should like it very much if you would now write the book on Financial Administration'. I wrote the book, but it did not get further than galley proofs for various reasons.

Then in 1985, John Offord Publications published a catalogue of forthcoming books, which included one by me entitled 'Finance and the Arts'. This reached page-proof stage and, again, for a variety of reasons did not reach publication. So, third time lucky?

Re-reading these previous manuscripts, I am aware that they are both out-of-date. In fact, it is quite terrifying that both accounts of how the Arts Council of Great Britain actually worked in the 1970s and how to tackle the finances of a performance company in the 1980s are now absolute history.

In a way, I am sorry that those books were not published since they would make interesting documents of social history. What is surprising is that there are still so few books available for students of arts management. The background as to why there are any such students should be recorded.

When I joined the Arts Council of Great Britain in 1957 the Secretary-General and I would walk from our offices in St James's Square to the Treasury Chambers once a year and make our bid for the following year's grant-in-aid. However, when what had been crumbs that had fallen from the Cabinet's table started to climb over the magical £1 million, the Treasury began to ask more searching questions. Particularly they wanted statistical information to support the arguments as to why the costs in the arts world were rising higher than the Retail Price Index and, also, why each year the Arts wanted so much more subsidy.

However, back at my office, if I were to contact the Hallé Orchestra or the Birmingham Repertory Company for detailed financial arguments about the relationship between, say, publicity and marketing expenditure and box office returns, or the cost of productions in terms of scenery, costume, acting and technical salaries, I would be told that all their funds went on to the stage or concert platform and they could not afford an administrator or accountant. "However, we have an out-of-work actor who does our wages every Tuesday and you could contact him..."

This was the reason I went to my Chairman and eventually the Council, with a case to launch a one-year Diploma Course to train some arts administrators.

My proposed syllabus, dated May 1967, was published as an Appendix in the Report of the Committee of Enquiry into training arts administrators published by the ACGB in 1971. My Chairman, the late Lord Goodman, approved the syllabus, and suggested purchasing a house and launching such a course. However, I was determined to place the course in an academic and arts environment; but no University or Polytechnic in the country showed any interest or response to my approaches. Then, first the Polytechnic of Central London (originally Regent Street Polytechnic) and then the City University picked up the cudgels.

A one-year course for trainee administrators of artistic organisations was launched in 1971 on the basis of contributions from the Polytechnic lecturers on Economics, Law, Statistics and Accountancy and I introduced guest lecturers from opera and dance companies, orchestras and drama companies. But it was like mixing oil and water. A lecturer in Economics from the Business School used examples from a raincoat factory whilst the 18 students had to reconcile this with what they were learning in the next session from a drama director or conductor. Luckily the students on that first course were astute enough to meld the course together.

The next stroke of luck was when we found Professor John Pick, who was responsible for laying the foundation for the Department of Arts Policy and Management at the City University. Little did we know that these first steps into training Arts Administrators would lead to the world copying us. I spent annual visits to Harvard where a Summer School was launched to teach arts management, then other universities commenced courses in North America and Australia and many M.A. and B.A. arts courses started to include Arts Management as a subsidiary subject.

It has always been of concern that what started out as a training course to provide properly trained administrators sorely needed by all the performing companies, resulted in a proliferation of professionally trained arts managers who ended up having to create hundreds of jobs for themselves with Regional Associations and other ancillary organisations developing a whole mass of bureaucratic methods of administering subsidies for all kinds of social courses not really at the heart of creativity – art in prisons, drama in schools, poems on trains, music in social clubs – but then you can read on in some of the following pieces as to why I regret money being channelled for these purposes and away from creativity.

But back to where we came in at the start of this introduction. All these courses in Arts Administration have found that there are very few books on the subjects included in the syllabus.

However, many of these subjects have been covered in my lectures as a Visiting Professor to the City University as well as in my articles published in *The Stage* and *The Guardian, Daily Telegraph* and other papers. Many of these articles have been copied in response to students' requests from all over the world and so it was thought it would be useful to collect the ones most in demand under one cover. It is hoped that the new introductions to these articles will set each into perspective rather than attempting to revise, rewrite or update them.

Many other theatre topics are also explored in response to all those questions I am constantly being asked, such as: "I want to be a producer. Can you recommend a book on the subject?" and "I have written a great musical. What do I do now?"

Of course the answers to such questions can be to urge such aspirants to learn by 'sitting next to Nelly'. There is admirable training for a producer by working in a production office, even though there are thousands of hopefuls attempting to obtain their first foot on the ladder.

My editor, Paul Webb, has asked very shrewdly who on earth am I to be giving such advice and how did I start in the business? My readers deserve to know that I started by leaving Sheffield University to join a touring repertory company, the Gateway Players, on the Isle of Wight. I arrived there one midnight to find that they were desperate for an actor to go on the next night at Shanklin as Mr Pym in *Mr Pym Passes By* by A A Milne. I had misled them about my work as an actor because I had, in fact, only appeared in amateur productions at school and university. At school in Manchester I played Sir Thomas More to Henry Livings' Cromwell in *Traitor's Gate*, and this only convinced me of my burning ambition to become an actor.

Whilst at school in Manchester I very much admired Joan Littlewood's work at the Library Theatre there, and I wrote to her to ask if I could join her Theatre Workshop group. She replied asking me to attend for an audition, with a P.S. in her own handwriting: 'please bring your plimsolls'.

I am sure I was ghastly as Mr Pym: my colleagues in the company swiftly realised I knew very little and accordingly taught me the rudiments of make-up and how to learn the part in a few hours before going on to replace a sick actor.

I had more time to prepare for the following productions and was pleased with three weeks' rehearsal to appear as the young Cameron in *Mary Rose*. I was still obviously inexperienced as an actor but seemed to attract the attention of young girls in the audience in Ventnor and Ryde and, eventually, on the mainland in Portsmouth. It was there that one of those rare opportunities presented itself when a talent scout came backstage after the show and asked me to join the Liverpool Playhouse Old Vic Company, a subsidiary company to the Old Vic in London, similar to the Bristol Old Vic. The director in Liverpool was then John Fernald, before he went on to run RADA, and I was immediately asked to play in *Julius Caesar*, alongside Eric Berry and Manning Wilson. My mother was from Liverpool (and my father from Manchester) so they were thrilled to attend my first night at Liverpool Playhouse.

My parents had been appalled at my having left university to become an actor. My father was a violinist with the Hallé Orchestra and my mother had been a soprano, so both were very much hoping I would not go into the hazardous show business profession. However, in Liverpool they agreed that if I managed to survive for twelve months as an actor they would then support me financially to go to drama school. My work in Liverpool went to my head so in very little time I made the rash decision to go to London 'to see my name in lights'.

This is when the harsh reality of show business hit me. I found some theatrical digs in Camden Town and trudged around the agents. I obtained a few odd weeks work, for example playing Crabtree in *The School For Scandal* at Farnham Castle Theatre, but slowly the money ran out. I knew that I could go home to Manchester with my tail between my legs but, as only a stubborn youngster could do, I stuck it out. And when the money finished I slept on a seat on the embankment until moved on by the police. I managed to spin a loaf of bread out for nearly a week, again being moved on when I tried sleeping at Euston Station.

Finally, through hunger and despair I went into an employment agency on the Strand who were amused to be asked whether they had a job for a young actor. Instead, having established that I was reasonably good at arithmetic, they offered me a temporary post as a junior audit clerk to a firm of Chartered Accountants in Cavendish Square. After a few weeks there the senior partner called me into his office and suggested I might consider becoming a clerk articled to him for five years at £500 a year. In those days one had to pay a substantial premium to obtain articles but here I was being offered a salary, no doubt more than I was then worth, but pegged for five years. I asked him for time to consider. "How long?" he asked. "Well", I suggested, "by 2p.m.?"

I walked round Cavendish Square, considered my alternatives, thought how happy my parents would be, and went back and agreed to sign articles. At 15 I might well have shot myself at the idea of becoming an accountant. However, I was soon captivated by the art of constructing a Balance Sheet and, at the end of five years, I completed the exams successfully and became a Chartered Accountant.

No sooner had I qualified than I left to become Finance Director to a Company owning optician shops, an optical works, the Curzon cinema and ultimately the Comedy Theatre. But that is a story for later...

1 THEATRE ROLES

Becoming a Playwright

The main thrusts of Tony's two articles on becoming a playwright are the need for patience, for perseverance, and for targeting. Plays take a long time to put on, playwriting is an art that one improves at, and there's no point in sending a play script to the 'wrong' producer.

The articles published here were written twelve years apart, but their basic message is the same, and continues to be as relevant today – and always will be. The only thing one might take issue with is the idea of putting your first dozen scripts in the bottom drawer. With plays, as with novels, the hardest part of a writer's career, after leaping (or sometimes, as it feels, just about dragging yourself) over the first hurdle of getting staged/published, is to follow up the first success with a second one. A surprising number of people may have one play or book in them, but hardly anyone has two, let alone three, that the public will pay good money for. So it may be that it is in the first dozen plays you write that the only one with a chance of making it can be found.

The first hurdle in getting a play on is, obviously, writing it. For this you need an idea, and time. The idea that you can dash off bits of plays in twenty-minute snatches on the tube or the bus is a romantic myth. As with any area of life there is always an exception that proves the rule, but essentially any form of writing needs time. Facing the proverbial blank sheet of paper is always a problem, even for very experienced writers, but once you get going you'll find you get on a creative roll, and you need the time to give full rein to this when it happens. The time of day when you write is, to quote Lady Bracknell, 'immaterial' but that you need several hours at one 'sitting' is essential.

It is said that there are only about seven basic plots in the world, but whatever the subject of your play, and whether it is based on a factual person or event (like Alan Bennett's *The Madness of George III* or Michael Frayn's *Copenhagen*) or is completely fictional, what will be unique about your play is not so much the plot or the subject matter, but your voice as a writer, the reason why you want to tell a story and the way in which you tell it.

Once you have come up with a finished script you have something to send to a producer. As Tony writes, the choice of a producer is essential – there's no point sending a drama to a producer who specialises in, and usually only ever stages, large-scale musicals. And vice versa.

In the 1988 Stage article, Tony refers to the fact that he and his colleagues 'read every script sent to us'. Don't be lulled into a false sense of security by this – this is highly unusual. Most producers get a huge pile of scripts thudding onto their floor every day and, even if they employ a reader, the likelihood of any particular script coming to the attention of, let alone being read by, a producer is minimal. This may be unfair/unreasonable/wasteful of a nation's talent, but that's the way it is.

The chances of any script being taken seriously are vastly improved by it being submitted to a producer via an agent, though even then there's no guarantee it will be read. So how do you get an agent? The Catch 22 here is that without seeing your play (agents don't read every play sent to them any more than producers do) or your being able to attach amazing reviews to a C.V. and copy of script/s when trying to get taken onto their books, how is an agent going to know about you or be interested in your work?

As so often in other areas of theatre, this is where the Fringe comes to the rescue, in that playwrights and actors can be seen and reviewed entirely on their own efforts, working together as individuals or forming theatre companies to stage a particular play or selection of plays. This all costs money but it also provides valuable experience and, as importantly, public exposure of your work.

When sending a play to a producer, preferably via the agent you have finally managed to secure (and *Contacts* will have a list of them), you will need to have patience. Plays, as both articles suggest, take time to stage, and six months or so is a reasonable time to wait for a theatre to become available, a star to read and accept the script (and have time to appear in it), and for the producer to raise the funds to stage the play.

There's no point in writing a play specifically tailored for an individual star, because if they can't or won't play the role, then the project will fail. Any play of artistic value will be playable by several people. It may be helpful to suggest particular actors for particular roles on a wish-list basis when submitting the script (though it will look better if you leave that to your agent), but it is the producer's role to find the actors, so setting down a list may prove to be counter-productive in terms of your relationship with the producer. If they like the script and arrange to meet you they will, in any case, ask you whether you had anyone in mind, even if only as a conversational gambit, and that's the time to mention any particular names.

One major issue, about casting to bear in mind is the numbers involved in any play. *Lost Horizon* was an over-ambitious plan and would have been at any time (unless you happened to be Ivor Novello), but these days the commercial pressures on producers are staggering, so the smaller a cast the likelier it is to be staged. It isn't a coincidence that the longest-running and/or most popular straight shows (i.e. non musicals) in the West End in recent years have included *The Woman in Black* (two actors), *Art* (three actors) and *Stones In His Pockets* (two actors). The only theatres likely to stage plays with casts of eight or more actors are the subsidised ones, principally the National – although Thelma Holt is a notable and courageous exception to this rule, as when she staged Noel Coward's rarely-seen *Semi-Monde*, with a cast of nearly 30.

If you can write a play which tells a story with six or fewer characters, then you are in with a stronger chance. Another help is to have a director and/or designer interested in the play. Again, there's a fine line between showing to a producer that the play is already arousing some interest – in that a director is potentially 'on board' the project – and irritating the producer whose role it is to arrange that sort of thing himself. All too often, writers (as well as the general public) tend to think of plays in terms of writers, actors and directors. Designers, lighting designers and, where necessary, sound designers, are also very important, and if you can show evidence of having given them some thought then you'll have further ammunition when it comes to fighting you way past other writers' scripts into the producer's In tray.

The other major point touched on in the articles is the need for a producer to match a play to a theatre – an issue that crops up several times in the course of this book, as it is a crucial consideration in staging shows. While this is principally an issue for the producer, there is a lot to be said for a writer researching theatres as closely as should producers. Every West End (and Fringe) theatre is different. If you can factor in the size and atmosphere of the sort of theatres where your play is likely to fit then, again, your piece will have an extra edge over its competitors. This doesn't mean a sort of painting-by-numbers approach to writing plays, but it does mean an awareness of the crucial importance of the performing space to the production of a play.

Soho Theatre in Dean Street, Soho, London, is technically a Writers' Centre as well, and offers writers' workshops and courses. This, and any similar programme organised by other theatres, is very useful for new writers – not necessarily in terms of writing plays but certainly in terms of how the theatre industry works and how best to market your work.

One thing about plays that doesn't seem to get mentioned, and this is the case with Tony's two articles as well, is that once a play has been accepted, other people begin to work on the script. If it is staged at a major subsidised theatre there may well be a dramaturg allocated to the work (a dramaturg is someone who in essence liaises between writer and director, who helps make a script workable as a practical piece of stagecraft).

In the commercial theatre you are unlikely to have a dramaturg to work with, but the director and, in rehearsal, the actors, will have an impact on your play. This is why writers are often not just invited to, but expected to attend rehearsals, so they can act on suggestions to adapt/improve the script, to make it more workable. This is not a case (hopefully) of people needlessly butchering your script, and a certain amount of re-writing should be seen as a normal, and helpful, part of the creative process.

True, some writers refuse to allow any changes, and will point out, to an actor in rehearsal, that the script indicates a comma rather than a full stop, so will he/she please phrase the sentence accordingly, but only writers with the status of living legend can – or are allowed – to operate like this, so don't get ideas above your station.

Finally, a word of encouragement. Writers may sometimes seem to come last down the food chain in the theatre world, but they are absolutely essential. There's no play without a writer, and although there are now thousands of plays that producers can stage and actors can perform in, there will always be pressure to stage new plays, so people are always looking out for new writers. Just as most actors are unemployed (a feature in the career of even a leading performer), so too only a handful of writers will be able to make a decent living out of writing plays. The rewards – in terms of sense of achievement as much as financial – are immense, and for anyone with a love of theatre the chance to be part of a theatrical community centred on a play, and to have actors perform your words every evening, is a marvellous thing. Getting there is not easy, takes time, involves set-backs and last-minute disappointments, but is, ultimately, well worth the effort.

PW

Your latest letter from someone sending scripts to producers (A F Southall, August 4th) asks yet again how aspiring playwrights can gain an insight into 'how the system works'. Naturally, they are concerned to know that their plays are read, their tapes heard, responses sent and, at least, scripts returned. All reputable managers are equally concerned about these matters.

My colleagues read every script sent to us and listen to all the tapes, even though this constitutes a great deal of time in the evenings and at weekends, month in and month out. It will not be surprising to readers of these columns to know that 97% of what is received is totally unproduceable. Even when it is not rubbish, most of it lacks craftsmanship.

Certainly it is useful for playwrights and composers to follow the history of individual producers to ascertain whether their primary interest is in drama, comedies, musicals, revivals, classical or avant-garde theatre, and so on. This is not difficult to do and saves a great deal of unnecessary heartache when a producer of touring modern comedies has to return large-scale musicals destined for Broadway!

What is difficult to convey to aspiring writers and composers is that even when one finds a rare good script and/or score, it all takes time. Firstly, as a producer one usually has to convince one's immediate colleagues that the script is worthy of all the attention of a full-scale production. One needs a committed team to be wholly supportive from the outset. Secondly, one has to gather around the project a director, designer and at least leading artists who make the product a saleable commodity to investors. Even, for example, a one set, six character play can these days require £150,000 - £200,000 to produce at a proper West End standard.

This may sound comparatively easy to a writer who is naturally convinced that his/her piece is an obvious winner that demands to be seen. However, the importance of time these days cannot be over-emphasised. A producer must consider that a production from the date of deciding to proceed to the final night of, say, a nine-month run on tour and in London, can take a year of one's life. T S Eliot's "I have measured out my life in coffee spoons" takes on a whole new meaning as one gets older! After reading the script of *I'm Not Rappaport*, Paul Scofield telephoned to say he was captivated with it and went on: "I'm busy until next April and then I can give you a year of my life".

As one gets older this is how one looks at these projects – a Peter O'Toole can spend three years of his life making *Lawrence of Arabia*, but even six months for him in a West End play now he is in his fifties can take a lot of convincing argument.

And not only the stars. It is an enormous sacrifice of Sir John Gielgud, Dame Peggy Ashcroft, Sir Alec Guinness or Dame Wendy Hiller to appear even seven times a week in a West End play for six months – but they fully appreciate that there is little chance of recovering one's capital in less than six months. But try persuading other actors to sign for six months. There were two small but very show-piece parts for young actors in *I'm Not Rappaport* which the director, Dan Sullivan, and the dramatist, Herb Gardner, required to be cast by exactly the right players.

It seemed disgraceful that all too many teenage actors on our shortlist declared they would not consider signing for as long as six months. Even when they had been 'resting' for up to a year and had never appeared on Shaftesbury Avenue, let alone with anyone as distinguished as Paul Scofield, they still declared they might miss a film or television contract so would never consider committing themselves for as long as six months. How can one ask an artist like Paul Scofield to re-rehearse every two or three months with new, young players who will not commit themselves? How long does a dramatist commit to a new play without even a salary? It was interesting to note that Helen Montague advertised auditions for replacements in *42nd Street* adding that 'no one need apply unless willing to sign a 12 month contract'.

A further universal problem is having to wait for the right leading artists. I have had a number of plays which have waited two or three years for the correct casting and I know that producers of the calibre of Michael Redington have waited years for the perfect casting of *Pack of Lies* or *Breaking the Code* or *The Best of Friends*. I always admired Colin Brough for closing the smash-hit play *Rose* at the Duke of York's when Glenda Jackson's six-month contract ended. He was convinced he could not replace such perfect casting and would rather end the run. The same thing happened when we could not find an adequate replacement for Paul Scofield in *I'm Not Rappaport*. Obviously there are many plays which can cope with repeated replacements (like *Hello Dolly*'s regular change from Carol Channing to Pearl Bailey to Danny La Rue!) but there are some subtle pieces of exact characterisation which it would be unfair on West End audiences to change if it resulted in an inferior production.

This is not to say that more than one actor cannot play Rappaport – it has been produced the world over since the London production, just as there have been hundreds of Hamlets. However, a new production of *Hamlet* with Daniel Day Lewis is a different matter from asking him to replace, for example, Kenneth Branagh in the Renaissance production.

Of course, there are some producers who will rush into a production without necessarily waiting for the perfect casting and it is up to the playwright and director as to whether they are content to sacrifice a perfect production for an immediate production and take that chance of success or failure.

Finally, there is the choice of theatre. Every London theatre has a style of its own and certain productions fit that style and attract the audience. However, certain shows fit uneasily into certain theatres and would have done better in different theatres. A few years ago, Theatre Projects attempted to put together a deal to present Mickey Rooney and Ann Miller in *Sugar Babies* at the Victoria Palace. It seemed absolutely appropriate for that show to be seen in what is essentially London's best burlesque house – the home of the *Crazy Gang*. However, the availability of the right theatre is as great a problem as the availability of the right artist, and the show is now going into that grand theatre – the Savoy. No doubt it will prove to be a box office success – but one yearns to see it in its right setting and one will never know now how much bigger a success it might have been at the Victoria Palace. But one can't always arrange everything to perfection and one has to compromise. *Rappaport* would have looked better in the Queen's Theatre but we had to settle for the Apollo.

Some producers now book the right theatres months in advance and some theatre owners are resourceful enough to keep the house available for that show. Thus, Her Majesty's was kept dark for months waiting for *Phantom of the Opera* and the Lyric is now closed until *Dry Rot* opens in September. The short-term contracts of artists also contribute to this phenomenon: thus Michael Gambon's *Uncle Vanya* must close at the Vaudeville in November and the next production there is already booked in (Ian McKellen in Ayckbourn's *Henceforward*). Likewise, *Hapgood* must close in September because the three leading artists' contracts expire and Rowan Atkinson has long-planned to return to the Aldwych (the scene of his successful *Nerd*) in *The Sneeze*.

But although it is understandable that London landlords book shows into their theatres months ahead, there is a growing disastrous practice whereby landlords of regional theatres housing tours book shows into theatres many months ahead for producers before a show is ever agreed. Thus perfectly good product ready for the road is turned down and tours cancelled whilst dates are being kept for managements who have yet to choose a play, cast and rehearse it.

So, Mr Southall, even if your new play lands on my desk tomorrow and proves to be a masterpiece, it is now unlikely to reach a West End opening until the Spring of 1990. This is all very sad for the theatres and no doubt is the reason why so many playwrights turn to television where nowhere near the same craftsmanship is demanded and the same number of hours of creativity is not required – you don't need to preserve the Unities – and when your characters have said what the need to say you just write 'fade'....there is more money there and a larger audience, and so what if your play is forgotten tomorrow like today's newspapers. That is how the system works.

Script For Success

The Stage, 14 September 2000

In 1988 I wrote an article for *The Stage* about the enormous hurdles to be overcome from the time a script or score is acquired by a producer until the time, often years later, when the first night is reached.

Since then I have been sent many hundreds of play scripts and musical scores, all of which I have read, and most I have returned with a critical reaction, 90 per cent being impossible to produce.

I have to admit that when I was 15 I was totally absorbed by the novels of James Hilton and I adapted *Lost Horizon* as a stage play. I sent the script to Henry Sherek, a leading play producer. He returned it with a letter to explain that "when a producer opens the first pages and finds that there is a cast of over 1,000 and 53 different scenes, including one recreating Shangri-La, it is unlikely that he will read much further…"

Now, nearly 60 years later, I too am reading scripts and listening to musical scores and wonder why so many of these creators spend so much time (and often so much money) on these submissions. So what can I advise?

Certainly many of the pieces I receive appear to have been written or composed by people sitting down with a blank sheet of paper and the determination to write a musical (or a play). But the few really superb pieces are ones that have screamed out to be written. If a theme is bursting forth, the creative team should also ask themselves again and again in which format it should be expressed.

You should also know in great depth the arts and entertainment world. A composer of a new musical should be steeped in everything from *White Horse Inn* to *Guys and Dolls*, and know what has been done before. It is no good if a producer knows that all the critics will immediately note that it is, even innocently, a rehash of old material.

It is dangerous to generalise, but often one finds musicals that have a single-minded overall creator. One soon realises where the music is merely there to service the lyrics and has no originality in its own right.

One other criticism is the tendency to have too elaborate a book. I would urge writers to study the economy of a musical of a long novel like *Les Misérables*, or even the sheer brilliance of *Art*, where three actors can, in one and a half hours, leave an audience feeling they have had a fulfilling evening.

My last piece of advice is to put your first dozen scripts in a bottom drawer, by which time you might be nearer to writing a success. There is nothing more dispiriting than a writer waiting for his or her one piece to be accepted before writing a second piece. I have been sent a play which was very poor but showed promise. I returned it with an exhortation to keep writing. A second play was little better, then a third, then a fourth and finally a fifth which was superb. So keep at it!

Becoming An Angel

The Stage, 15 July 1999

It may seem inconceivable that the basic financing of the world-renowned West End theatre depends on no more than a couple of hundred private investors known as 'angels'. Productions of plays now cost, in 1999, in the region of £200,000 and musicals anything between £1 million and £3 million. Most producers seek to raise the capital cost of a production from their private list of some 50 or 60 investors who are expected to stay committed to a producer, just as the producer is usually expected to offer units of investment in all his (or her) productions to his regular investors.

Once a production is planned, the producer must prepare a budget both for the total cost of a production up to the first paid public performance (i.e. the capitalisation) and the subsequent weekly running costs and likely weekly box-office income (at various levels of seating capacity at a chosen theatre). These budgets are included in investment brochures sent out to 'angels'.

Investment units can vary from about £250 each to some £10,000, and a producer can reserve the right to take offers on a 'first call' basis or, sometimes, can scale applications down if a production is over-subscribed. However, if a production is under-subscribed the producer is responsible for the balance of capital required. Simple investment contracts are exchanged between a producer and each 'angel'.

If there is a weekly surplus of box office receipts over running expenses this is accumulated until it is reasonable and safe for the producer to begin repaying investors a proportion of their investment. If and when the whole capitalisation has been repaid (i.e. 'recoupment' has been achieved) any subsequent 'profit' is usually divided 40% to the producer and 60% to the investors pro rata to their respective investments. However, it is certainly not unusual for the capitalisation not to be 'recouped' in full and any such loss is then borne by the investors who may receive back only a proportion, or even none, of their original investment.

It should be noted that although the producer receives no share of the income until after the costs of the production have been repaid, the producer is entitled to charge a weekly management fee for the office administration and accounting work necessary to support a production. It is also becoming common practice for the producer to receive a royalty for the creative input required to assemble a production.

Apart from the weekly costs of hiring a theatre, paying the technical staff and theatre employees, advertising and publicity charges and paying the performers, there are royalties to be paid (usually a percentage of box office receipts) to authors, composers, directors, designers and others in the creative team. Very often such royalties are calculated in two tiers: a lower one to assist in keeping costs down until capitalisation is recouped, and a higher one once the production is in profit. This two-tier system may also apply to the rental charge by the theatre owner.

Investment contracts now carry a paragraph warning about the high risk of investing in theatrical production. This is because, unlike the stock market world where shares and dividends might fluctuate over the years, all or part of the entire investment can be lost in a short time. Furthermore, it can take weeks or months or even years before even a successful production goes into profit. Thus it is wise for any investor contemplating regular investment to spread it over a wide 'portfolio' of, say, five to ten productions and to limit investment in each one to a specific maximum sum (say £500 in a play or £1,000 in a musical).

A producer may sometimes feel able to offer investors a small share of other revenue, such as royalties from foreign productions, tours or cast albums.

When the production finally closes, the accounts will certify the final production accounts to investors.

Further information on theatrical investment may be obtained from the Society of London Theatres (SOLT, 32 Rose Street, London, WC2E 9ET, tel. 020 7557 6700).

Good luck to all prospective investors.

Theatre Management

Tony's article on Theatre Management identifies the importance of theatre managers – or house managers as they are often called – a reflection of the fact that theatres are frequently referred to as 'houses' – hence the 'house full' sign outside a theatre once every seat has been sold, or the phrase 'papering the house', which means giving away free tickets so that the theatre looks fuller than it would otherwise be – something that often happens on press nights or if a play is having a dip in sales but the producers want to get people in to see the show in the hope that word of mouth will spread the news that it's a good show and worth seeing.

The 'front of house' is the public area of the theatre – everything in front of the stage – the box office, the foyer(s), restaurants and bars, the auditorium (seating area) and so on. This makes up the initial point of contact between the public and a play or musical, and the successful management of this experience is crucial if people are to enjoy the night at the theatre.

There are two schools of thought on theatre management: the old fashioned one (and nothing necessarily wrong with that) is that it is best to have experienced managers who will have been in the theatre business for twenty years or so and will have, crucially, both the experience and the air of authority to deal with the public – a public that can often be a nightmare, especially now that general standards of behaviour have sunk to their present deplorable depths. True, theatre audiences are generally better behaved than cinema ones, but the overall level has certainly been noticeably lowered in recent years.

The more modern school of thought is that if theatre is to be seen as fresh, engaging and 'relevant', and to attract the young people it needs, then it should have appropriately young theatre managers, to whom people can relate. This is a valid argument on one level but ignores the fact that (rightly or wrongly) most theatregoers are middle-aged, so will feel more comfortable with a middle-aged manager. Also, many young people expect the theatre to be rather different from 'normal' life and will expect to see a dinner-jacketed middle aged man in the theatre foyer. It's all part of the image.

Despite appearances – largely created by the dinner jacket and the theatre architecture – there isn't, these days, a great deal of glamour about theatre management. As a profession it offers those interested in theatre a great opportunity to work in the industry, but the days when it was also a satisfying administrative career in its own right are largely over, unless you reach the rarefied upper-levels of the profession as a General Manager.

Theatre management essentially comes down to the two 'l's – light bulbs and loo paper. The theatre manager has to ensure the former are working and the latter is in plentiful supply. The numbers of loos are something he can do nothing about, and Victorian theatre architects seem not to have worried over-much about the provision of loos for women, hence the long queues outside the ladies' at most theatres during the interval.

Managers also have to ensure that there are enough ushers to check tickets, show people to their seats (though that is a courtesy rarely observed today) and to be present on health and safety grounds to evacuate the theatre in case of emergency. They liaise with company managers to ensure that everyone is seated – as far as possible – before the performance begins, and to ensure people are re-seated by the end of the interval. They will welcome VIPs, ensure that backstage facilities for the cast are in working order (more loos and light bulbs) and that the public areas of the theatre are clean and tidy.

Unfortunately, they rarely have any direct authority any more over many of the areas for which the public assumes they are still responsible. The box office is no longer under their direct control but is part of a centralised structure, and they no longer hire and fire box office staff. Given that this is where most of the immediate problems (double bookings, missing tickets, etc) occur during the stressful and pressurised half hour before 'curtain up', the fact that the manager isn't actually in charge but at best can liaise with the box office is a major problem. Similarly, cleaners will be employed on a contract basis by a head office rather than the Manager, whose only direct area of authority (usually) is over the hiring of ushers.

All this makes the job of Theatre Manager far less satisfying than it once was, in the days when they actually managed their theatres. If the press represents, as Kipling once observed, 'power without responsibility' then today's Theatre Manager often seems to have responsibility without power.

The context of Tony's article was that Managers are nonetheless a very useful barometer for producers and theatre owners, as it is the Managers who are there in the theatre every night, taking the temperature, as it were, both of the show (are the cast getting jaded? Is X forgetting his lines? Has Y upset everyone backstage?) and of the public – what are they saying on the way out? And at the intervals? What sort of people is the show attracting?

Owners and producers should heed his advice, as these are indeed people with their finger on the pulse. Young people can be as astute and as competent as older people, and everyone has to start somewhere, but there is still a lot to be said for having experienced people in this crucial position of authority. The downside is that after twenty years of dealing with unreasonable behaviour by members of the public – some of whom have to be experienced to be believed – Theatre Managers become weary and jaded with the whole experience, and are simply clinging on to their jobs. They, like doctors, have traditionally taken to drink to cope with the stress – but then, equally traditionally, drink has fuelled the theatre as much as it ever fuelled Fleet Street, and many a difficult West End opening night has been made bearable by a stiff gin and tonic in the Manager's office once the house is safely seated and the curtain gone up.

So spare a thought for the person in a dinner jacket standing in the foyer as people swirl about him: he may look serene but he'll be wondering how to break it to the electrician (who traditionally also does the plumbing) that the men's loos need unblocking yet again, as soon as the curtain goes up, while two of the ushers need replacing from somewhere tomorrow as they've just handed in their notice after being shouted at once too often tonight by stroppy customers. Perhaps Gordons' or Beefeater could sponsor a Theatre Management training course or two?

PW

Theatre Management

The Stage, 20 February 2003

One is always hearing about the plight of producers, the problems experienced by box office staff, the crises of technicians or the difficulties of attendants and usherettes in dealing with the public. But no one pays much attention to the troublesome times which House Managers have, possibly because one sees them in dinner-jackets front of house and thinks what a wonderful job it is to stand there beaming at the public before and after the shows eight times a week.

However, this veneer of quiet respectability covers a difficult job, working long hours, often underpaid. It is all very well for one to cite the easy hours of, say, 10 a.m. to 1p.m. and 6p.m. to 11p.m. but what does one do marooned in the West End every afternoon, except for matinee days?

Also, often being the licensee for the bars and ultimately dealing with every aspect of the public's attendance is quite a responsibility. Not only the financial responsibility of daily sales but the legal responsibility of public liability problems.

Above everything else is the very real concern of not having any sort of Employees Association to turn to for advice and assistance. After all, SOLT can represent its individual members and the Theatre's Management Association can act for Employing Companies which can join. However, theatre managers cannot join TMA and have no recourse to any similar body.

Repeatedly, *The Stage* columns report on the tremendous work achieved by the Peter Tods and Michael Graysons of the profession. But, in the last resort, we can be losing some of our best theatre managers who are the vital nightly link between the public, the producers and the production artists and technicians. It is the theatre manager who brings together all the elements that make a performance work.

Yes, I know that Peter Tod and Michael Grayson did not leave their theatres as House Managers but they were excellent examples of how House Managers can grow into knowing and loving every pore of every brick of their theatres so much so that they will instinctively know what shows will be successful in their venues.

Woe betide a theatre landlord who does not regularly consult his House Manager about their audiences and artists and future programming, hours of performances and cleaning staff and bar arrangements. It is, after all, the House Manager and no-one else who is the pivot between the production, the house and the audience.

But the real problem is that not only have theatre managers no trade association to assist with advice and support but there is no possibility of any assistance with compensation for loss of office or financial support when out of work. I should be interested to hear from anyone about any benevolent society or charity to which a sick or destitute Theatre Manager can appeal. So far as my investigations go, there is no professional support for the breed we call Theatre Managers, although there once was an organisation called the Entertainment Managers' Association: and what happened to that?

Television Stars and the Theatre

The Stage, 20 May 2001

Former soap star Martine McCutcheon's recent illness which necessitated her missing performances of the National's *My Fair Lady* has given the tabloids lots of column inches devoted to questioning the commitment of stars to their stage productions.

But to understand this typical problem one needs to debate both the standards of our current professional training of artists and the readiness of theatre, television, film and radio to engage performers without any training.

We are constantly being torn by arguments in favour of controlling entry into Equity because of the appalling percentage of actors who are regularly unemployed, and whether this should be achieved by restricting admission only to those professionally trained in the way that doctors, lawyers and accountants are. After all, the theatre is regarded as a profession.

On the other hand, there are arguments used by those opposed to any restrictions of entry pointing to outstanding performers who have emerged from the amateur stage or from 'discovery' programmes such as those hosted by Carol Levis, Hughie Green, Jane McDonald and Matthew Kelly. But then I often wonder how many present stars once worked at Selfridges but one would not recommend a London store as an obvious channel to stardom.

The problem with our present tendency to award star status to soap actors or pop singers is that there is a real danger that they can injure themselves or their voices and also that audiences can be disillusioned.

Some of the essential ingredients of professional training are to ensure that artists not only learn to perform and act well but that they can sustain such performances. Thus we have the problem that producers of television soaps have too little money to employ actors, so they cast to type.

The performers simply play themselves and have not the slightest notion of what someone like Alec Guinness could achieve playing a complete family in the film *Kind Hearts and Coronets*, or Laurence Olivier playing in both *Oedipus Rex* and *The Critic* each night in the theatre. Further, these artists could sustain eight performances a week for months on end.

Recently, an American colleague expressed his concern that Elaine Paige could only perform six times a week while Gertrude Lawrence played eight times per week even when suffering a terminal illness.

Then there is the widely advertised appearance of Dannii Minogue in *Notre-*

Dame de Paris, but just try to find out which performances she will decide to play. Further, it was hardly fair to investors and audiences that Richard Wilson refused to play the mid-week matinee of *The Weekend* at the Strand Theatre.

The essential professionalism needed to sustain eight performances a week, month in month out, was not always provided solely by the leading drama schools. Alternative training was available in the dozens of regional repertory companies stemming from the twice-nightly weekly seasons to the higher levels achieved by three-weekly reps. It was all too easy to scoff at the weekly reps but the grind of spending mornings rehearsing next week's play, afternoons learning the lines for the week after next, followed by 6.15 and 8.30 performances of this week's play, gave young actors the basic commitment on which to build a career.

These days a youngster can be picked off the streets by a television talent scout and herded into a soap opera – indeed, *Soapstars*, ITV's planned follow-up to its phenomenally successful *Popstars* series, will even allow viewers to follow the process.

In this environment it is certainly not the fault of the artist that professional demands become impossible to meet.

Finally, there is the current problem of inaudibility. Most of our theatres were built with perfect acoustics so it is rarely the fault of the buildings. Certainly until recently our theatres did not need any artificial amplification and sound engineers. But, even so, many West End productions have young actors who simply cannot project their voices.

Not long ago Ian McKellen was asked by a Hollywood movie director, "Still shouting at night?" which showed not only contempt for the theatre but ignorance about voice projection in live performances.

It is all very well to hear actors currently at the Old Vic, the Haymarket and the Lyric when speaking normally, but whenever the script requires a lowered voice or whisper they become completely inaudible. Yet Paul Scofield could toss off an aside in *I'm Not Rappaport* which could be heard clearly at the back of the gallery, or Ralph Richardson could peel an onion at the end of *Peer Gynt* muttering as an old man and still his voice winged to the furthest walls of the theatre.

This is what a well-trained professional actor can and should be achieving, even months after the director has departed from the production.

It is quite different in television. A recent gunshot in a television documentary followed by a close-up of a cow's eye and then its mouth dropping did not leave an audience thinking, 'What a wonderful performance the cow gave', but, rather, 'That director should win an award'. In the theatre it is the actor who matters eight times a week.

2 PERFORMING ARTS SCHOOLS

It's Got to be All or Nothing – The Schools for Performing Arts

The Stage, 19 April 1990

Those who have read about what the new Schools for Performing Arts are intending to achieve know that it is to train young people towards a profession that now requires performers to sing and dance and act and play instruments and use the modern technical facilities which are at the heart of the new British musical theatre embodied in *Cats, Les Misérables, The Phantom of the Opera, Aspects of Love* and *Miss Saigon*. The latest American musicals such as *Barnum* have also put new demands on artists.

Cameron Mackintosh and Nicholas Hytner had to scour the world for artists with training adequate enough to play in *Miss Saigon* and continued to advertise worldwide that they are prepared to pay artists to retrain for 12 months so that they will be capable of taking on some of the roles. There is therefore an obvious chasm in the existing training provided by the leading schools and what producers will require. Certainly if an artist aspires to becoming a Fonteyn, a Gielgud, a Domingo or a Menuhin, one goes to colleges such as RADA, the Guildhall School, the Royal Ballet School or the Royal College of Music. But where does one train to become a Michael Crawford who can sing in *Phantom*, act in a television comedy series, tight-rope walk in *Barnum* and now star in a new film?

If one doubts the need for such schools that we intend to launch, let them take note of the disastrous new production of *Show Boat* at Stratford-upon-Avon which combined the efforts of Opera North and the Royal Shakespeare Company, two of our leading opera and drama companies. One hopes that the production, to be recast and re-rehearsed shortly for a season at the Palladium, will iron out some of the performance problems.

At Stratford, the house lights darkened and the conductor slid the orchestra into the overture. No one paid much attention to this pedestrian selection of popular melodies as there was no real sense of theatre. It needed a spotlight on the conductor and a re-orchestration of the overture to avoid the titters of the audience with the old-fashioned odd intervention of the chorus.

The curtain rose on one of the worst sets I've seen for years – certainly last time I was on the Mississippi levee it did not look like a warehouse in Wapping. The whole production was hampered by this dismal and cumbersome set, which moved around without any motivation readily discernible to the audience.

Six of the leading roles were shared by singers. No doubt eight performances a week of an opera are too taxing on principals, but *Show Boat* hardly falls into that category. Indeed, when Cleo Laine was singing 'Julie' eight times a week for six months at the Adelphi, she still managed some Festival Hall recitals on Sundays. Perhaps the current artists alternated because of other commitments – they certainly did not seem committed to *Show Boat*.

But the really great problem with this production, which reared its head again and again, was the inability of the superb Opera North singers, the Royal Shakespeare production team, the Northern Philharmonic Orchestra and the Opera North chorus to cope with a musical. One had hoped that the British theatre had now learnt that musicals are an art-form in their own right. It is no longer a case for the Jack Hylton Repertory Company going up-market or the English National Opera going down-market. The dabbling in popular music, even by great opera singers, is nearly always disastrous, as was Maria Ewing's Prom performance last season at the Albert Hall.

It is perhaps unfair of me to pick out Jason Howard's Gaylord Ravenal except that his performance typified nearly all the other leads in *Show Boat*. I do not question this superb baritone's success in *La Traviata*, *The Marriage of Figaro* and particularly Faure's *Requiem*, but he is not and never will be Gaylord...It is perhaps unfair to cite Howard Keel in the 1951 travesty of a film version, but at least this showed Gaylord to be a devastating charmer who can with one verse of 'Make Believe' sweep Magnolia off her feet. Of course he's a scoundrel and a wastrel, but his overwhelming charm must come through both in the acting and the singing. This performance made Gaylord seem like a Soho pimp in *The World of Paul Slickey*.

Perhaps the fault was the conductor's since the whole pedestrian strict tempos which grinded on like a Victor Silvester Come Dancing band ruined songs like 'Make Believe', 'Can't help Lovin' Dat Man', and even an impossibly slow 'Ol' Man River'. Maybe I'll be told that this is exactly how Jerome Kern wrote them and intended they should be played in 1927. But audiences have changed and musicals are not and should not be museum pieces. Anyone who has heard the Soliloquy in *Carousel* knows it needs to be sung with conviction.

'Ol' Man River' is the same and although the packed audience at the end clapped along with the music, like a Max Bygraves record, this song should tear your heart out. No doubt I'll also be reminded that the audience obviously enjoyed a jolly evening, but *Show Boat* fails unless, as the curtain falls, there isn't a dry eye in the house. In this connection, unlike in opera, the conductor should be subservient to the artists and not to the orchestra and the score. Perhaps this is why opera conductors do not like conducting ballet and musicals, where the sense of theatre must dominate the performance.

The costumes (at times a garish combination of reds, oranges, purples and violets) did not always add to the atmosphere and the pristine and well laundered whites of the 'coloured folk' did not give any impression of the sweat and grime of 'darkies all workin' on the Mississippi'. Even the bales of cotton appeared untouched by human hand and Joe's rolled up sleeves and shirt open to the waist appeared so calculated, and not because he was working hard in the heat.

All this criticism really saddens me. But the point of it all is not whether this particular production is good or bad, it is that the whole production and performances missed the point of musicals needing a style of performance totally different in text from opera, ballet or drama. The artists, singers, dancers, musicians, even lighting and sound technicians need to be steeped in the very special panache which is what musicals are about. I should perhaps here mention Simon Green who showed, as in *Follies*, that he knows exactly how to perform such songs as 'Goodbye My Lady Love' with a swagger that was the very heart of the cake-walk.

Danny Kaye in *Two by Two*, Tommy Steele in *Singin' in the Rain*, Michael Crawford in *Barnum*, Barbra Streisand in *Funny Girl*, Liza Minnelli in *The Rink* – none of them could sing particularly well by Opera North standards, none could dance as well as Royal Ballet dancers, nor act like Royal Shakespeare actors – but they brought a brilliant artistry to the profession which is great in itself and a thing apart.

This is also why it is regrettable that opera companies, no doubt because of box office considerations, have to resort to poor productions of Lehar and Cole Porter, Friml and Rodgers and now even Sondheim. I have long considered that the Arts Council, instead of subsidising two opera companies in London, one each in Wales and Scotland and one in the North of England, should have encouraged one of them to become a 'musicals' company on the lines of the light opera company in Vienna which includes *Annie Get Your Gun* in its repetoire. It might take some decades for such a company to develop style enough to play six nights a week of *Frederica, Carousel, A Tree Grows in Brooklyn, A Waltz Dream, Pacific Overtures* and *New Moon* or how about *Oklahoma!, Veronique, Company, Student Prince, Bloomer Girl* and *Bubbling Brown Sugar*?

Aficionados of Viennese operetta like Charles Osborne will tell us that this art form is very different from what aficionados of American musicals like Mark Steyn will tell us is what they are about. Maybe we can go on splitting these differences into ever smaller categories but what we do know for starters is that they are all a million miles from opera and ballet.

No doubt it will take the new schools for performing arts some years to blend satisfactorily the basic academic curriculum and the performing arts training sufficient to produce artists to cope with such a repertoire. It certainly took three to four years to achieve a similar successful blend for the department of Arts Policy and Management at the City University. The hard-core training in finance, law, economics and statistics fitted uneasily alongside classes in how to run orchestras, young people's theatre, dance ensembles, arts centres, art galleries, theatres and museums. But The M.A., Ph.D., M.Phil., B.A. and Diploma courses at the City University now train some 150 people a year and have led the world to copy them with similar courses in North America and Europe.

Nearly all the graduates obtain jobs before the end of their courses with the enormous expansion in all art forms, technical facilities, training and administration in the arts, entertainment and leisure industries worldwide. This is why it is so exciting that this country is now launching the Schools for Performing Arts hopefully on the right lines.

Chairman Sets His Site On Fame

The Stage, 19 October 1989

A great many confusing statements have been published in various daily and weekly newspapers recently about the so-called Fame school, so that it would appear useful for everyone to have a brief, accurate history of how the various parties came to be involved in this exciting venture.

The original concept, pioneered by Mark Featherstone-Witty, led to the formation of the Schools For Performing Arts Ltd. I was pleased to be asked to be the first Chairman of this Trust, since I had already seen two similar projects fail to proceed. Whilst I was Finance Director of the Arts Council of Great Britain, the then Secretary-General, Sir Roy Shaw, and I met Tommy Steele about the possibility of establishing a school for performing arts on a site in Soho. Andrew Lloyd Webber was also reported as having visions of such a school being developed within the site of the Palace Theatre.

However, here, at last, was the possibility of creating a school which could respond to the current needs of the present arts and entertainment industry. Since the end of the World War II, Great Britain has created an international standing in the performing arts, which is pre-eminent, because it is the outcome of many specialist schools. Our magnificent talents of singers, dancers, actors, musicians, directors, composers, dramatists and technicians have largely flowed from such schools as RADA, LAMDA, the Guildhall, The Royal College of Music, amongst others. However, these are all post-18 schools.

Further, for all the brilliance of the talents stemming from these schools, the whole new stream of British (and American) musicals, such as *Cats*, *Les Misérables*, *Aspects of Love*, *The Phantom of the Opera*, and *Miss Saigon* has put a great strain on the new style of talents required from performers. It is no longer simply a matter of being a supreme ballet dancer or actor or jazz musician or opera singer; one has to be able to sing and dance and act and play instruments and deal with the sound and lighting technology and even tightrope walk (for *Barnum*).

It was to meet the new demand that the philosophy and new curriculum for the Schools for Performing Arts Ltd was established, and attracted the flow of star names as our patrons with a view that this support would be for a national programme of schools to be launched in a number of cities in Great Britain. Cameron Mackintosh recently joined as a Patron, precisely in the knowledge of his problems alone in casting and re-casting his musicals.

All this has required the input of hard work donated by all our Trustees over a period of seven years. This culminated in the British Phonographic Industry Trust donating £2.36 million towards the cost of launching the first of such schools and the Department of Education and Science responded with an additional £3.54 million.

At this stage, the London School for Performing Arts and Technology Ltd. was incorporated (known as The BRIT School) to administer the first of such schools on a site at Selhurst, offered by Croydon Council. LSPAT is a completely separate and different company from the Schools for Performing Arts Ltd, and our Patrons.

The investment of some £6 million in the first school, being launched in Croydon, is a major national achievement. It is hoped that another school may be established in Liverpool, spearheaded by Paul McCartney, in collaboration with the SPA Trust.

The confusion which has recently been caused locally in Croydon emanates from local political and educational issues which the Croydon Local Authority will need to resolve. However, the Schools for Performing Arts Trust is enormously grateful to the profession and, in particular, to its Patrons who have endorsed and continued to support our new national philosophy of approach to education in the performing arts and technology.

3 THEATRE CATERING

Theatre Catering - an Introduction

Given that the social side of theatregoing is a major part of the experience – and, when it comes to corporate entertaining, it could be argued it's the main part of the event – it's surprising how little attention most theatres seem to pay to their catering.

Tony's article mainly addresses the issue of food – that theatregoers don't want or need to sit down to a 'proper' waitered meal, but need a faster-moving buffet instead. It remains the case that most London theatres fail to provide anything remotely like this sort of service.

This is partly a matter of size – most theatres were not built with an integral restaurant area; only the Royal Opera House and the London Coliseum enjoy this facility in a major way. However, the Royal Court, since its late 20th century refurbishment, has had a very good restaurant, and the Lyric, Hammersmith, also has one. All except the Lyric expect customers to sit and have their orders taken by waiters, so Tony's point about speed/convenience of service still stands. The Playhouse, on the Embankment, which has changed hands several times, used to have an attractive if slightly crowded restaurant area as recently as the 1990s but at the time of writing that service is no longer on offer.

True, you can buy sandwiches at the Coliseum and Royal Opera House, but they are very expensive: what is needed is simple, nourishing and affordable bar snacks. For many older theatregoers that idea will conjure up an image of Joyce Carey and her rock hard cakes behind the station buffet in the Noel Coward/David Lean film *Brief Encounter*, but given the plethora of coffee shops serving muffins and cakes of every description, it shouldn't be beyond the wit of theatre managements to arrange a similar cheap, quick, filling (albeit fattening) snack for customers who have rushed to the theatre after work and need something to keep them going until they fall into a restaurant after the show.

Food is one thing; you'd think drink was easier to provide.But here again, the general standard of service in West End theatres is very poor. The problem is two-fold. Firstly, there simply aren't enough staff. However good a barman/woman may be, two people to service a long bar packed with customers before a show or in the interval simply isn't enough. Given the very low pay, it's extraordinary that management doesn't provide more staff, and that customers don't make so much fuss that management has no other option but to up their staffing levels. It only costs up to £20 to pay a bar person for an evening: the cost of some four or five drinks. An extra pair of hands would quickly pay for itself and make a disproportionate improvement in level of service and customer satisfaction.

This lack of staff even happens on press nights – the one time when you would think a theatre management (or, if necessary, the producer) would splash out £40 or £60 and get some extra staff in, yet I have been in a well known London theatre on a crowded press night with one not very bright barmaid allocated to the stalls promenade bar as critics and customers jostled to stay upright in the struggle to get a drink before the five-minute bell went at the end of the interval.

The second issue is the calibre and training of bar staff. Theatre managements seem to prefer to have young people behind the bar. This may look sexier than some cockney old dear, but believe me, the 'old girls' who used to be an inevitable fixture in any theatre bar were more cheerful, more charming and – despite the received wisdom that everything old is worse than everything young – more efficient.

As it happened, they would often (though not inevitably) subscribe to the idea of 'perks' and pocket the occasional 50p. It's for this reason that managements introduced electronic tills behind bars, doing away with the far simpler and vastly quicker method of bar staff simply putting cash in a dish or on a tray and settling up once the customers were served and the incoming or interval was over.

This may mean that the very minor pilfering that used to happen no longer does, but it also means that it takes a ludicrous amount of time to be served a (very expensive, so who's doing the ripping off in any case?) drink, as anyone who has ever stood furiously by while some slow newcomer has to have the till operation explained in the middle of the interval) by another member of staff (if you're lucky) who ought to be serving the customers rather than engaging in ill-timed training procedures.

If this sounds rather impassioned, it is. A drink at the theatre should be a pleasant way of preparing for, or having refreshment from, a play or musical, and a chance to anticipate or discuss it with your friend/s. That it is, routinely and with very few exceptions, an unseemly, sweaty, stressful scrum is a constant blight on theatregoing, and Tony, never one to pull his punches, could have laid into theatre owners with greater vigour on this issue. If everyone complained to the manager, loudly and unpleasantly, on the way out of the theatre, something might eventually be done. Customers have nothing to lose but their queues.

PW

Introduction to Theatre Catering

I find it slightly alarming that I am writing about my article on this subject published in 1992 and that nothing much has changed in the past decade.

Whilst it is heartening to have seen Lottery funding going towards the cost of rebuilding and refurbishing many of our subsidised theatres it is being left to the wealthy theatre-owners, Sir Cameron Mackintosh and Lord Lloyd Webber, to find the finance to renovate their West End theatres. But there are many other West End Theatres owned by landlords who have not made money out of world-renowned musicals. These are mainly our drama houses which have missed out both on lottery funding and commercial profits to help refurbish their buildings.

What is even more troubling is that all this money has gone into and is still going into the fabric of theatres – admittedly sorely needed - but none has been available for creativity.

Many of us have been shouting warnings that the loss of revenue money to encourage new playwrights will come home to roost; and it now has. I cannot remember a time in the past half-century when the London West End classified list has been so short. There is at the time of writing (mid-2003), no inclusion of ten theatres and the West End has only two new British plays being staged. This is a disgrace and London should be ashamed of this catastrophe.

Just compare Chicago which has nearly 200 theatre companies in existence and has a theatrical scene as exciting as any city in the world. There are so many world premieres available there in the next couple of months and playwrights, actors and directors flock to that city. Plays can be produced there so cheaply that producers are attracted to present new plays and audiences delight in flocking into their theatres without feeling it is an event.

I know that barely a decade passes without a journalist writing that the theatre is dying. Others will point to exciting work being achieved by the National and Royal Shakespeare companies and by the few fringe theatres. But unless something is done and done quickly to inject fresh inspiration into the West End commercial drama houses we shall see there a cemetery of revivals, one-man shows, look-alike pop stars and a few Hollywood names in American plays.

The few American visitors we have attending London theatres still complain about the price of our programmes, the cost of drinks in our bars and our poor theatre catering which is usually limited to sweets, chocolates and popcorn. All right, American theatre seats usually cost more than those in the UK but then the programmes are free there and not the £3 one has to pay to receive the same monthly RUG theatre magazine inserted in all their theatre programmes.

There remains the constant feeling that once in a theatre one is being constantly coerced into buying over-priced drinks served by surly youngsters who have no experience or sensitivity to being in a theatre; they might just as well be working at Chessington Leisure Centre. When our arts management courses urged our theatres to become more commercially minded we did not mean them to become the mindless mausoleums we now have to experience.

It is thirty years since I was at the Arts Council of Great Britain analysing which regional theatres ran their catering at a loss and which at a profit. Our results found that of those restaurants run in-house 50% ran at a profit and 50% at a loss. Of those franchised out 50% ran at a profit and 50% at a loss. What was apparent was that all those running at a profit were operated by a management which was steeped in experience of running theatres rather than MacDonalds.

West End theatres usually have too little room to organise any catering beyond drinks. But occasionally one can be surprised by what can be achieved in a small space. Fifty years after the Mermaid proved one can run a theatre restaurant and make a profit, the Old Vic is now successfully running a stylish restaurant in its downstairs bar. Its mouth-watering menu is available 12 noon to 2 a.m. six days a week. What is more, their front-of-house staff seem to enjoy their work and know about their theatre. Perhaps the regular appearance in the building of stars such as Kevin Spacey and John Malkovitch adds some spice to their work, but certainly playgoers appear to be welcomed and not simply tolerated.

Cameron Mackintosh indicated at his recent press conference about the new look he was intending to bring to his seven West End theatres, that this customer attention and economic pricing of tickets and bars will be at the forefront of his thinking. Let us hope that all this rubs off on some of our other theatres.

Theatre Catering

The Stage, 15 October 1992

Sooner or later, theatre consultants are asked the dreaded question about whether or not to franchise certain activities, most particularly catering.

It is surprising that so many people are ignorant about the work of theatre consultants and assume that they are independent bodies brought in solely to resolve management problems. However, the bulk of the work undertaken by Theatre Projects Consultants is a consequence of its senior staff having worked for up to 40 years presenting plays and musicals in most West End commercial theatres as well as those commercial and subsidised theatres all over England, Scotland and Wales. Thus, there are no problems in giving advice on theatre design, seating and sightlines, backstage get-in and get-out requirements, lighting and electrics, stage management and technical requirements, sound and acoustics, dressing room and rehearsal requirements, chorus and orchestra accommodation, box office facilities front-of-house management and company structure. There are also the design requirements for catering and bars to service the public, staff and artists. However, which of these services might be franchised out is a different problem. It could, of course, be held that commercial theatre landlords franchise out production requirements to professional producers, whereas subsidised companies are responsible for their buildings as well as their productions.

Nevertheless, whilst running a theatre is usually held to be as much part of show business as presenting a play, many companies consider that catering can be classified as a quite separate activity. Hence, many years ago the Arts Council undertook a survey of the merits and demerits of franchising out catering. I seem to remember that about half the subsidised companies remained responsible for their own catering whilst the other half franchised out this activity. Of those who ran their own restaurants about a half did so successfully and the rest proved a failure. Of those franchised out about half proved a success and the rest a disaster.

Thus, the question is 'dreaded' because, being no statistical proof that any one method is better than another, a consultant has to resort to the seemingly inept 'it all depends…' response.

Those restaurant and catering activities run in-house were successful where the theatre had an imaginative and experienced house manager employing an equally innovative and professional catering manager who was capable of exercising efficient stock control. Together they could provide exactly what theatregoers require, whether during the day for morning coffees when booking tickets, lunches before and afternoon teas after matinees, pre-theatre dinners or post-performance suppers. Successful theatre catering provides quick, hot and relatively cheap risotto dishes, goulashes and stews for a fast-moving, self-serving queue of those rushing from their jobs at 6.00p.m. and needing to eat before a 7.30p.m. performance. Unsuccessful in-house catering usually stems from poor stock-control and too many concessions to staff. Nothing breeds staff bitterness more than seeing ruthless economies to productions whilst legs of lamb are known to be going out of the back door.

Good franchising results can be achieved by using a catering firm already successfully responsible for other theatres' catering. I have already tried my best not to cite particular examples but I have to mention the swift, successful and appetising, hot, self-service meals at the Wolsey Theatre in Ipswich. Also of particular note is the recent excellent innovation at the National Theatre, the Terrace Café, where you can choose one or more dishes from about 15 hot and cold starters – a quick and easily controlled service both by the caterer and by the consumer.

All these compare favourably with a recent visit to the Crucible, Sheffield, where a superb production of *Cabaret* was marred for me by my hunger. Having arrived at 5.45p.m. after a long journey, I found the restaurant geared to a three-course dinner service and there was a quick-service snack-bar where the waitress announced: "Sorry, we ran out of food at 2p.m!"

Unsuccessful franchised catering often provides a waitress service and three-course dinner with wine, which is rarely required, often expensive and takes too much time, let alone inducing sleep during the ensuing performance. Even worse is the outside caterer attempting to apply too much attention to a possible market between 7 and 10 p.m. to non-theatregoers who, at worst, can cause noise during a performance and clutter bars at intervals.

When I was at the Arts Council not only did I promote the causes of taking on such additional arts forms as jazz under the aegis of the music department and photography under the art department, but I also suggested, perhaps half-jokingly taking on the art of cookery. After all, as Michael Grade has explained about programme-making in his recent McTaggart Lecture, it is a process governed by the cannons of art rather than the laws of industrial mass-production. "There are more economical ways of doing it, just as painting by numbers is a more economical method of producing a picture than trying it Rembrandt's way". I should like to have told that to Elizabeth David had she been Chairman of an Arts Council Cookery Panel!

All this has not even given attention to the details of any contracts to be signed with outside catering firms. Does the theatre require a flat rental or, more appropriately, a share of gross takings or net profits? As with the productions themselves, it is always better for both parties to be involved in the financial success of the venture so that they can apply their joint efforts to it.

Of course, franchising need not be confined to theatre restaurants alone but can also be applied to the bars, the programmes, ices and confectionery, cloakrooms and even to the box office facilities. The problems here start to be compounded. The legal and financial burdens placed on the House Managers, particularly by local authorities' licensing laws, require that experienced personnel should be responsible for the safety of hundreds, even thousands, of playgoers in a public building eight times or more a week. Having such a senior manager on the site before, during and after every public performance is inefficient if that person is not then also to be made responsible for other activities and services.

Nothing is more frustrating to a theatre-goer than to appeal to the manager about certain services only to be told that the bars and their staff are the responsibility of a catering firm 200 miles away, the box office and its staff responsible to a head office only open at 10 the next morning, the programmes the responsibility of a publisher 50 miles away, the sandwiches produced by a local caterer, the ices supplied by a national ice-cream firm in another country – one is tempted to ask, "Well, what on earth do you hold yourself responsible for?" Of course, an experienced manager will not attempt to deflect all responsibility, but shrewd playgoers easily discern where a theatre has become as automated as many of our cinemas, i.e. more intent on selling popcorn and hotdogs than paying attention to the quality of watching films during the sounds and smells of people eating. Unlike cinemas, theatres present live shows and are a people-orientated service. The film character coming down from the screen into the audience still remains a romantic fiction of Woody Allen's *Purple Rose of Cairo*, but live actors have remonstrated with audiences as audiences have heckled actors. Actors also require the House Manager to respond to their needs if they are to give their best during performances, just as playgoers expect a standard of personal service in a theatre where presenting plays and musicals must remain a successful vocation and not an unsuccessful industry.

Thus, it ain't what you do but the way that you do it!

4 THEATRE PROMOTION

Introduction to Ticket Prices
The following two articles were published in 1990 and 2003, both dealing with seat prices at theatres. Obviously the prices have changed over the years but the ratios and arguments remain the same.

Directing a New Course
The Stage, 5 June 2003

When Laurence Olivier worked with Dustin Hoffman in 1976 under John Schlesinger's direction of *Marathon Man,* it was reported that in one scene Hoffman had to arrive breathless. In rehearsal, Olivier was surprised to be kept waiting whilst Hoffman ran round the set three times in order to arrive out-of-breath: When he arrived on set duly breathless, Olivier asked: "Have you tried acting?"

On reading the past few months' journals on various arts management subjects I have come across countless courses on such subjects as audience development and innumerable schemes suggesting how to finance the publicity and marketing departments. There have been Arts Council subsidies set aside to encourage youngsters into the theatre or to urge ethnic minorities to take a special interest in drama. One is tempted to ask, "Have you tried good, new plays?".

I recently attended the Lyric, Hammersmith, where I sat in a packed and enthusiastic audience responding to the Shared Experience production of *After Mrs Rochester.* This dramatised story of Jean Rhys was a marvellous piece of theatre, now continuing its tour to Cambridge and Guildford. What brought this audience out to Hammersmith? Simply, a moving and thought-provoking play superbly produced. Visiting friends from abroad earlier this month asked me to recommend a new British play and I had to admit there was not one on in any of the 45 West End commercial theatres.

Whenever I examine the launching of a new theatre group and its successful development, I am always impressed by the simple fact that it was the result of its creativity.

American Group Theatre in 1931 to the English Stage Company at
Court in 1951 the emphasis has always been on the plays and the
n. Surely the recent resurgence in cinema-going has been the simple
better films?

The fascinating story of the Group Theatre in New York charts the cultural
growth of American theatre at that time. The Group's work was developed
out of such playwrights, actors and directors as Clifford Odets, William Saroyan,
Irwin Shaw, Franchot Tone, John Garfield, Luther and Stella Adler, Maxwell
Anderson and Sydney Kingsley. It led to such Broadway transfers as *Golden
Boy, Awake and Sing* and *Waiting for Lefty*.

Similarly, the English Stage Company was first developed out of the work of
George Devine, John Osborne, Tony Richardson, Oscar Lewenstein, Angus
Wilson, and other creative artists and went on to the success of *Look Back in
Anger*, Noel Coward's translation of Feydeau's *Look After Lulu*, Olivier in
The Entertainer and other inspired pieces of new creativity.

Critics and journalists continue to debate what they consider to be the
problems for all the arts and entertainment world in the forthcoming year.

The first problem they cite is the lack of teenagers at theatres and concerts
which they attribute to the apparent formal atmosphere of show business.
Then they criticise high seat prices, always quoting the top prices at Covent
Garden Opera House. Further, they also urge Arts Council funding to be made
available for educating young people about opera and classical music as well
as to extend theatre audiences to bring in ethnic minorities, the unemployed
and the disabled.

Pardon me if I feel all this is a trifle déja-vu. When I started going to the
theatre in 1933 I was told that it was good to see a youngster there as audiences
were growing older. It is probably true that the narrowing of the range of seat
prices is of concern.

I have used these columns many times before to urge producers to increase
the price of front stalls and reduce the price of gallery seats. In the case of the
recent production of *Mrs Warren's Profession,* the gallery at the Strand was
closed when it should have been filled by young playgoers revelling in a Shaw
play for, say, £1 each. I was certainly happy to pay two shillings to see C.P.
Snow's *The Affair* from the gallery at the Strand in 1961.

There will always be people who prefer to see their Shaw on film or television
or DVD and not only because of accessibility. Similarly, the pop industry is
having to contend with those who want to hear their pop by downloading it

from the internet. This has not stopped EMI re-signing Robbie Williams for a sum reported to be in the region of £50 million just as Cameron Mackintosh signs on Alex Jennings to play Higgins in *My Fair Lady*, even though the film is available on television or DVD. There will always be an audience for Robbie Williams live at Wembley Arena just as there is one to keep *My Fair Lady* at Drury Lane for three years.

Should we be alarmed that there is such a small percentage of our population who go to live performances of concerts, plays and musicals when we should be grieving that Arts Council funds, which should be invested in creativity are being channelled to extending the composition of our audiences? Do we really want to go down the same road whereby museums and galleries give up their roles as thought-provoking experiences and turn themselves into popular theme parks purveying entertainment while losing their essential elements of appreciation and discovery of art and history?

Should we be concerned that Arts Council funding goes to opera companies that demonstrate that they are 'developing new audiences' instead of encouraging the emergence of a new Benjamin Britten whose work will be available for future audiences? Similarly, should the television and radio industries be developing their technology such as the new digital signals which are not proving attractive to the general public, when this money could achieve so much more if spent on new and better programmes to replace the endless repeats, reality shows and the development of celebrities who have never had a day's training in their lives?

This month Greg Dyke, the BBC Director-General, presented a film to BBC staff across the country explaining his five-year campaign to raise the standard of culture at the BBC. Dyke has nailed his colours to the mast and his target is to make the BBC the most creative organisation in the world. He has said that: "the only purpose is to make better programmes with better content".

Live theatre should take note of this and instead of increasingly finding ways to lure non-playgoers into theatres, simply apply themselves to producing good new plays and musicals.

Ticket Prices – Seat Price Shuffle

At the 2nd International Congress on Managing the Arts promoted by the International Society of Performing Arts Administrators in Amsterdam in June 1988 I criticised the trend over the last few decades for theatres and concert halls to narrow their seat-price range.

To my surprise, the next day the London Financial Times (25th June) ran a front-page article by Barry Riley on ticket touts at Wimbledon which cited the problem: "Exactly why commercial promoters of overbooked shows such as *The Phantom of the Opera* do not price to market I am not sure…there can be no sympathy for failure to take account of market forces."

When I started my intensive theatregoing in Great Britain in the 1940s (to drama, opera, ballet and concerts) I found that generally the top ticket prices were ten times the cost of bottom ticket prices. In London's West End most shows were priced from 1/6d (now 7.5p) to 15/- (now 75p) or 2/- (now 10p) to £1. I well remember that audiences considered the move from 20p to 40p or 60p was a major decision and an important theatregoing step – from the gallery to the upper circle or from the upper circle to the back of the grand circle.

Nowadays, most theatres in the West End charge from £5 to £15 (for a play) or from £6 to £20 (for a musical). Thus the range of seat-prices has moved from a top-to-bottom ratio of 10:1 to 3:1 and this has also resulted in the narrowing of the difference between price bands. Audiences can be bemused at being asked to make the minor decision of purchasing a £10 rather than an £8 seat. In fact, most theatre and concert-going audiences have become so used to the perfect sight-lines and proximity of their television sets or the perfect acoustics of their stereo systems that they are not prepared to spend £20 on the costs of transport, babysitters and food and drink only to book two inferior £6 seats in the gallery.

Thus, we have the unhappy result that we have alienated the new, young, underprivileged audiences by monstrously over-pricing the cheaper seats and driven the top-priced seats on to the black market by monstrously under-pricing them.

This situation is even more critical on Broadway where many theatre seats are priced solely at $45 and $30 resulting in similar problems in that the price-range has been narrowed considerably in the past few decades.

If you spend time in a box office assessing reasons for the public buying tickets there are two main groups: the first asks for "two good seats in the front of the Stalls (Orchestra) – about the centre of row D or E", and if you ask them for £40 or £60 or £80 or £100 it usually does not affect them…they are seat-orientated because often they are taking business colleagues, or a wife or a girlfriend, or are part of a civic outing (a mayor or governor or board director)…often it is a social outing and they need to be seen in those seats – certainly if they are a tourist and have spent £500 on a visit to London or New York and they need to see the show in question. The other group asks for "two £6 tickets" and that is what they want – they are price-orientated and know that they cannot demand good seats in the stalls for that price.

Recently the box office at Her Majesty's Theatre in London opened booking for a Sunday charity performance of *The Phantom of the Opera* in July (in aid of Cancer Research) with the stalls and circle priced at £100. A queue formed for the opening of booking at midday and it sold out in just over one hour. And why not? The ticket touts landing like parasites on the TKTS queue in Times Square, or outside theatres sell tickets easily for *Phantom* (and *Les Misérables* and *Cats*) for prices of up to £100. Often these tickets are forged, the prices and the positions being altered - and even the dates. It is reckoned that ticket touts on these shows alone can make up to a quarter of a million pounds per year (and no doubt none of them pays income tax!).

If the market price for the top seats for *Phantom* really is £100, what are the reasons for selling them at £20 (£21 from October next)? The Financial Times states the touts 'thrive on mispricing and fill the gaps when others make a mess of running the primary markets.' Why should the creative team not benefit from the higher income rather than the touts – or the performers or even the investors who continue to take chances on new productions, bear losses and invariably put profits back into further ventures?

Much higher top prices would also enable promoters to bring down the bottom prices. I see no reason to charge more than £2 for the very high Gallery seats in most London theatres, with their restricted views of a distant stage and often imperfect acoustics. This would nurture the audience of the future which does not like to be patronised by having to queue for last minute tickets when they are reduced on production of students' cards. It would also help encourage the young married couples who seem to desert theatres, concert halls and galleries between their student days and the later, more affluent days in their 40s and 50s after their children have grown up.

Further, very high top prices enable one to offer substantial discounts on incentive schemes. It is no longer particularly attractive to offer discounts of 5%-10% but difficult to offer more unless individual prices are higher. It is time for investors' contracts to be drafted to enable more cross-fertilisation of audiences between productions. If the top price for West End productions were to be, say, £40 one could offer a substantial discount of 50% for those booking for four shows over a period of four months and still be receiving the £20 now being charged for many shows.

Of course, there are many British managements who will spend long hours thinking up all the many reasons for not doing anything about the current situation. There are those who think solely about top prices and cite the Royal Opera House, Covent Garden's highest price of £70 as the reason for a wide section of the population being excluded from opera and ballet. This wholly ignores ROH publicity that over 25% of its seats are below £8.

At international conferences it is invariably the experience of British delegates who return home brimming with ideas, that they then encounter a wall of opposition to any change in a world that is now advancing so swiftly that we shall soon be left behind in the field of arts and entertainment where, as in many other professions and industries, we should once again be taking a lead.

Theatre Size

Tony's basic premise in these articles is that there needs to be a wider variety of sizes of London theatres where young/new producers can cut their teeth, and where relatively small-scale productions, initially mounted (for economic rather than creative reasons) on the fringe can move into more economically viable half-way houses. In this respect he compares London unfavourably with New York, a city where there are far more venues available to producers, and where 'fringe' shows that take off can continue running in the same space.

The points he makes in these pieces are still very valid. New producers, for whom the idea of mounting a show (at about £250,000) in a West End theatre is an impossible dream, have only the option of staging something in a fringe theatre. This category of playhouse encompasses a variety of size from, say, the small but prestigious Jermyn Street Theatre with 70 seats to the Bridewell with about 150 (depending on the seating configuration) or the Riverside Studios in Hammersmith, with a maximum capacity of some 400 seats.

The problem with fringe venues is not just that they are in effect uneconomic – unless you have a one or two person show with minimal sets and 'effects' and which sells out for the whole run – but that you have to book them for set periods, so a play/musical that does well cannot extend its run and make its investors a decent return on their money. The other issue is that the national press is unlikely to review a show that only runs for three or four weeks, and virtually no one will review anything that runs for less than two weeks unless the subject matter is of particular appeal to a publication's editor.

Tony's 1999 article bemoans the loss of numerous venues that he knew in the 1940s: well, they have indeed gone, but then plenty of new venues, often following in the footsteps of Dan Crawford's ground breaking pub theatre, The King's Head, in Islington, have taken their place. But the fact remains, as he mentions in that article and the 2001 piece, that the new venues are not designed to be hired for potentially open-ended runs.

The answer, then, is not so much to find new spaces that can be converted into theatres, but to manage them in such a way that a longer (and therefore profitable) run becomes possible, and new producers – and their backers – can actually make a profit, as well as gaining crucial experience in managing shows that run – and need managing – for more than three or four weeks.

In effect this means finding companies or individuals who are prepared to let out empty spaces (as Tony suggests) for longish periods of time, to companies/ producers who themselves hope to stage shows for more than the usual three or four weeks. Were this to happen, London's theatre scene would be transformed, and the huge gap between staging a show on the fringe and in the West End would be narrowed.

PW

Theatre Size

The Stage, 4 November 1999

When I first started to regularly go to the theatre in London in the forties there was a wealth of venues where young producers could launch new productions. These included the Embassy at Swiss Cottage, the Granville at Walham Green, The Q Theatre at Kew and the Palace at Walthamstow, amongst others. Sadly, these venues are no longer operating. This is similarly the case with the larger suburban halls which have disappeared, such as the King's (Hammersmith), Chelsea Palace, Finsbury Park Empire, Wood Green Empire, Golders Green Hippodrome (now run by the BBC), Shepherd's Bush Empire, Streatham Hill Theatre and Kingston Empire.

There are no equivalents in London to the plethora of available venues in New York, known as the Off-Broadway theatres, the off-Off Broadway theatres and now even the off-off-Off Broadway theatres.

Most of these are tiny converted warehouses, churches, libraries and cinemas. They are available to producers and their great advantage is that they are ready to house unlimited runs. Occasionally, a big success Off-Broadway can transfer to a Broadway house, as was the case with *I'm Not Rappaport*. But the majority of Off-Broadway successes are allowed to run indefinitely in what is probably the most appropriate venue for them. Thus productions such as *The Fantasticks*, *And The World Goes Round*, *Nunsense*, *Forbidden Broadway* and *Party* have run for years in their small Off-Broadway houses.

However, the all too few off-West End theatres such as the Almeida, Battersea Arts Centre, Bridewell, Bush, Donmar Warehouse, King's Head, Lyric Studio, Jermyn Street Theatre, Riverside Studios and the Tricycle are all run, not by landlords, but by creative teams who seem to have no desire to house long, successful runs.

Bernard Miles built and ran the Mermaid Theatre on the basis of the policy of having a new production every five or six weeks. He used to moan that he took off his successes to put on his failures. This is the great problem when a creative team is running a theatre. Although Miles was able to arrange transfers of several big successes to the West End, such as *Lock Up Your Daughters*, *Hadrian VII* and *Cowardy Custard*.

There are also the rare transfers from small venues, such as *Mr Cinders* from the King's Head to the Fortune, *Romance, Romance* from the Bridewell to the Gielgud and the more recent Almeida transfers to the Albery.

But there are many small-scale productions which could and should be allowed to run their natural lives in their original venues.

Recently, there was a fascinating production of *Floyd Collins* at the Bridewell. Sensibly it was booked in for a fortnight as no one expected a musical based on a man trapped in an underground cave to meet with a big West End transfer. But, despite a considerable demand for seats for its last few performances, there was no opportunity to extend its run for what undoubtedly would have been a packed further three or four weeks, because a following show was scheduled to open. Show business being what it is, the demand for seats is an ephemeral phenomenon and a show often swiftly reaches a sell-by date. But bring it back three months later and that demand has strangely evaporated.

Similarly, transfers from across the Atlantic also have a sell-by date. Recently, a number of British hits have swiftly transferred successfully to Broadway, such as *Amy's View*, *The Weir*, *Art* and *Closer*.

However, in spite of criticism from America regarding the increase in the number of Brits on Broadway, it is difficult for British producers to acquire the rights to swiftly transfer New York successes to London. Six months ago the wonderful plays *Wit* and *Side Man* could have succeeded on Shaftesbury Avenue but the delaying tactics of some American producers have resulted in these plays losing their chance to become London successes.

Small But Perfect

The Stage, 15 March 2001

The many issues debated at the Theatre 2001 conference should be further explored regularly through the pages of *The Stage* without waiting for the rare occasion, however successful, of a major get-together.

One issue raised which was not taken up positively is the lack of small theatre spaces in the UK run by landlords and not by artistic directors. In New York there are some 20 Off-Broadway theatres, some 30 off-Off-Broadway theatres and 100 or more off-off-Off Broadway theatres. (Yes, these are officially advertised as 'off-off-Off'.) Some of these are run by artistic directors but the majority are available to new, young producers on a normal rental basis with an agreed get-out weekly box office figure. Thus, on the same basis as any normal Broadway or West End production, if a play is running successfully above this figure, neither the landlord nor the producer can give the other notice to quit.

No one can possibly overestimate the achievements of Jonathan Kent, Sam Mendes, Dan Crawford, Nicholas Kent, Carol Metcalfe or all the other British directors of Off-West End venues. The superb work at the Almeida and the Bridewell, the Donmar Warehouse and the Bush, the Tricycle and Hampstead has enriched the British theatre scene. Of course we are all short of funds, short of new plays and producers and investors, but these shortages could be assisted if there were some 50 new small venues run by landlords.

At present a new producer who finds a good new play might be able to scrape together investors to provide £20,000 or £30,000 to produce the work in a small space. But investors quickly withdraw when they hear they can only count on a three or four-week season because the existing venues are run by artistic directors who want to get their next show on.

Of course, the argument is that if a new production meets with that rare smash-hit status one can always then raise the other £100,00 to transfer it to a West End theatre. This has proved worthwhile on rare occasions. But generally the result is the same as the transfer of Sondheim's Company from the Donmar to the Albery where it lost all its capital investment. The recent successful production of *Merrily We Roll Along* was very specially directed for the Donmar and could well have run for six months there. Transfer it and this fragile achievement would crumble in a larger theatre with a different texture, and not just because critics themselves agree that they have different standards in reviewing a show in the West End to the very same show when it appears on the fringe, let alone a regional or studio theatre.

Of course a venue in receipt of Arts Council subsidy has a responsibility to produce a range of work during each financial year. Bernard Miles always maintained that at the Mermaid he took off his successes to make way for his failures.

When I worked at the Arts Council, I presented a paper suggesting that new venues should be made available for new work and the Council suggested buying the Shaftesbury Theatre, which missed the point of my argument.

Perhaps an approach should now be made to City insurance companies, large international finance houses, banks and conglomerates, many of whom have vast properties all over the country.

Most of these financial institutions will invest in works of art rather than ephemeral productions where their name dies at 10pm. They also invest in property and could well make it available to performing companies where the name of the institution might not be tarred by a creative work of which they may well disapprove. Some spaces are empty for long periods and could well house new plays.

In New York, landlords have converted churches and libraries, shops and brothels, cinemas, garages and warehouses into off-off-Off Broadway theatres let at a commercial weekly rental.

A small-scale success like *The Fantasticks* can run longer than *The Mousetrap* in its original venue without being forced to transfer. New products deserve this chance, new investors deserve this gamble, and new playwrights deserve to be seen, all for want of a home with the offer of an unlimited run.

How To Broaden the Appeal of the Arts

These articles can seem, on the surface, to be rather pessimistic; they argue that there's only so much you can do to bring the theatre to the people, or *vice versa*. Yet they also make the point that far more people go to the theatre than live football, and therefore, not surprisingly, theatre generates more money, in terms of ticket receipts at any rate, than football.

Tony deduces from this that it is pointless trying to make the arts more 'popular' as they already are: it's just a question of perception (as the word is now used) that makes them seem elitist or unpopular and therefore in need of being made more popular in their appeal.

His conclusion is that, rather than expose the maximum number of people to the maximum amount of theatre, we should accept that only a certain percentage (albeit a healthy one) of the public is interested in the arts, and that the best way to attract them to them, and to enable the arts to flourish in modern Britain, is to make the theatre that is on offer as good as possible.

The target, he suggests, should be quality of productions rather than quantity of theatre offered, and that theatre, far from being a 'service' which people expect as a right, is an art form that can only be promoted and performed by companies, centres of artistic excellence, whose results (productions staged) speak for themselves and to their natural audience.

The only problem here is who measures or rather, defines, artistic excellence. A small and 'unpopular' theatre company could arguably provide a more innovative, exciting and 'important' theatrical experience than the RSC, yet the RSC's excellence could arguably be demonstrated by its popularity and number of tickets sold. This brings us back full circle to the debate about whether accessibility and outreach equals artistic merit.

A more pertinent observation is that, even if every theatre and concert hall were to be filled to bursting point every performance, 'only' some 3% of the population could be described as attending live arts performances. Planners and allocaters of funds have therefore, he argues, to get over the idea that blanket coverage is a definition of a breadth of appeal when it comes to the arts.

What this leaves unanswered is not so much the initial question – how to broaden the appeal of the arts – but the measurement and management of that broadening process. One person's centre of artistic excellence is another's pretentious codswallop. Theatre cannot be entirely left to the marketplace – many of the most profoundly moving and/or entertaining plays seen at the National or the RSC would never be staged if left to an entirely commercial

theatre community – but ultimately it is ticket sales that mark the only demonstrable measurement of artistic success, however depressing this may be.
PW

How to Broaden the Appeal of the Arts I

Entertainments Business Monthly, June 1990

In 1957, the year I joined the Arts Council, its grant to the Old Vic Company was £12,000 and a survey undertaken by the Royal Victoria Hall Foundation discovered that "less than 0.01% of the audience were artisans". Over thirty years later, similar surveys of audiences have become that much more sophisticated and some have even responded to my demand to extend such surveys to include a review of why the majority of the population does not attend arts events.

Northern Arts is just about to undertake a new study and Greater London Arts has just completed similar research. All this money spent to confirm what many of us feel we have known for half a century. The arts remain an interest of a minority, most of whom are white, middle class and middle aged.

There is evidence that people are influenced by transport problems, safety after dark, access to arts buildings, the amount of exposure to the arts at school and at home, the expense of attending and so forth. If we were able to tackle the figures from the opposite standpoint, we would reach the same conclusions, but perhaps in a more logical way.

For example, if one calculates the total possibility of audiences in all the theatres, concert halls, opera and dance houses, galleries and museums one could possibly arrive at a figure of, say, 5 percent of the population of Great Britain who could physically be accommodated in the available venues. So, why are we surprised, given that no houses are filled 100 percent all the time, to find that only 3 percent of the population has ever attended a 'live' arts event?

If we examine the life-cycle of many individuals in audiences, we find that they commenced going to live entertainment in their teens, tended to stop attending when developing their careers and family units with their financial consequences, and returned to attending such events after their middle age.

I have always been amused to hear – continuously since I first started going to the theatre in 1932 – that 'audiences are getting older'. Since the average age then was about 45, the average age now must be about 103. Yet, of course, the average age remains around 45.

Next, the influence of transport. Surprisingly, this affects people's shopping and other habits. When the Arts Council devised its Bus Subsidy scheme in 1948, later a Transport Subsidy – by which eight or more people attending an arts event could have one half their transport costs paid – there were extensive surveys undertaken of catchment areas of theatres.

As for the problem of safety after dark, now where did I read about that? Tyrone Guthrie, in *A Life in the Theatre*, described the grand opening of the Royal Coburg Theatre in 1818 (now the Old Vic) as having to provide 'patrols of extra lights as much-needed protection for persons venturing into a district infested by pickpockets and the dreaded garrotters'.

The exposure to the arts at school and at home also seems to be part of preconceived notions of researchers. Why is it that members of the Boards of most of the City, commercial and industrial companies who ought to be sponsoring the arts, do not do so? After all they have mainly benefited from the very best public school and university education which has nurtured their appreciation of arts activities.

Yet they often end up with interests in hunting, shooting and fishing and prefer to spend their companies' advertising budgets at Ascot and Wembley, Henley and Epsom. I would suggest that about 5 percent of the population is intrinsically interested in, and devoted to, the arts while only about 0.02 percent of the population is intrinsically interested in fishing. Just as there are people born who love fishing, so there are some who love the arts. They come from all sections of the population. I have met them in prisons – for some years as a prison visitor and member of the Board of Wandsworth Prison – as much as in hospitals. They are to be found in supermarkets as much as in hotels; more so than in boardrooms it appears.

Naturally, education in the arts, for adults as much as for children, can heighten the understanding of them but, as T S Eliot maintained, appreciation should precede comprehension.

So is all this a recipe for despair? Not at all. What it does question is whether the Arts Council is correct in its interpretation of its Royal Charter's second object: 'to increase the accessibility of the arts to the public throughout Great Britain' as being a geographical problem to be resolved by more extensive touring in the regions. Sir Roy Shaw, when he was the Council's Secretary-General, emphasised that the Council's first chartered duty was 'to develop and improve the knowledge, understanding and practice of the arts'. Thus, greater accessibility can be attained through educational activity rather than by initiating more regional work. Indeed, Lord Goodman, when he was the Council's Chairman, once joyously proposed that such a small island as Great Britain could not afford to subsidise one expensive (Royal) Opera Company, let alone the English National, Scottish and Welsh National Opera companies and Opera North, and that it would be cheaper to pay the cost of flying our microscopic opera audiences to the New York Met by Concorde.

Surely this merely heightens the fact that it is comparatively unimportant that so few people attend live entertainment for whatever reason. Certainly those who wish to are nearly always undeterred by all the factors that the surveys list.

For example, I caused consternation at a Lord Mayor's banquet in Manchester once when I described it as: "A Cultural desert worse than Scunthorpe" – I was then invited to the next amateur Gilbert and Sullivan production in Scunthorpe.

My remarks were provoked by the closure of the Opera House, the Palace and the Hippodrome in Manchester, and the consequent desertion to London of the majority of my contemporaries from the sixth form at grammar school who were interested in the arts and show business.

It is significant that many of those moved back to Manchester with the re-opening of the Palace, the inauguration of the Royal Exchange and the revitalisation of the Hallé Orchestra. Indeed, at Theatre Projects we are regularly asked by certain towns and cities all over the world to recommend how best to provide new venues to house drama, music, opera and dance events specifically to attract a particular type of worker to an area.

Thus people whose interests lie in the arts and live entertainment tend to live where they are available, just as people interested in bird-watching don't usually choose to live in Piccadilly.

How are we going to make the arts more accessible if not by expensive touring or by artificially creating arts interests? Or, even more difficult, by transporting audiences to the larger centres?

In these days of modern technology it is perhaps primitive to think of making live theatre accessible to the remote areas of Cornwall or Northumberland and the results of attempting to do so are hardly likely to satisfy those of the local population who are interested. With film and radio, cassettes and CDs, DVDs, video and satellite television, everyone can be reached. Patently, it is not the same as live theatre, music, opera or dance: but what is the alternative? And more importantly, who is to be responsible for these decisions?

The really sad aspects of the Minister's latest plans for the future of the Arts Council is that they are based on the idea that provision of entertainment and the arts is a service. All the plans for Regional Arts Boards are as though the arts are to be provided by local authorities in the same way as sewerage and rubbish collection. It is greatly to be regretted that the current thinking in central government, indeed by all professional politicians and their servants, is not based on furthering the creativity in the arts. Obviously they have not read the first 20 Arts Council Annual Reports, fired with the wisdom, vision and creative knowledge that only the great artists then involved could generate.

When the English Stage Company was set up with what was then considerable funding no-one worried that an initial production of, say, *Look Back in Anger* played in a 397 seat theatre in London to half-empty houses. In the event, it transferred to the West End and to Broadway, was turned into a major British film and was seen in cinemas and on television and heard on radio, thus reaching many millions of people living far from their nearest theatre.

What mattered then to the Arts Council was that it was nurturing and fostering a climate in which new drama, music, opera, dance, painting and sculpture could be generated. All that mattered was that the work should be produced. It was then entirely up to other forces to take up the work and exploit it.

The responsibility was on local authorities and regional associations to disseminate that work. In a democracy it is entirely up to local communities whether to bother or not. The fact that East and West Sussex are jointly bottom of the table of the 39 English Counties' arts expenditure in 1989/90 is entirely up to them, and if they want to be 'free from the arts' then that is no doubt reflecting their electorate's wishes.

Accordingly, I suggest that the Arts Council should, together with the regional Associations and local authorities, draw up a list of the creative companies in drama, music, opera, dance, the visual arts, etc which shall remain the responsibility of the Arts Council. There probably are about 50 or 60 of them, large and small, each easily identifiable. These companies should be properly subsidised to do their job and should be assessed primarily for their artistic creativity – not measured by box office success.

There are but a handful of people in Britain capable of serving on the Advisory Panel needed to make such an assessment. The second list will be the clients who are predominantly 'service' companies who wish primarily to provide audiences with their basic, regular arts and entertainment fare. There are about 1,000 of these companies, large and small, and they can be assessed by Regional Arts Boards and also properly subsidised to do their job. The main criteria of assessment will be efficiency of management, production and box office success. There are a tremendous number of people – accountants, business managers, lawyers etc – in the regions capable of serving on such Assessment Panels.

It is high time, after over half a century, that we stopped pussy-footing around this problem. Everyone knows well-enough which companies fall into which category and there is no need to put up a smokescreen to blur the situation by citing the one new play produced by a 'service' company every other year, or the one commercial comedy included by a 'creative' company on occasion. There is simply no stigma in being in one category or another and we should put behind us the British snobbery on both sides of this fence. We have been fortunate to create an arts and entertainment industry which leads the world and no-one should be allowed to destroy it by implementing the present folly of proposals.

How to Broaden the Appeal of the Arts 2

The Stage, 28 August 2000

Suddenly this month plays, musicals and films are all attempting to bring together sports, the arts, social conditions and politics and one wonders whether this cannot be other than a good thing.

Certainly it is a good thing for the box office. The wonderful success of *Stones in His Pockets* can be measured not only by the weekly takings at the Duke of York's, but is reflected by almost every Broadway producer claiming to have acquired the US rights of this two-hander about the commercial rape of a remote Irish village by a Hollywood film unit. Now the film rights have been sold it will have come full circle.

We are about to be drawn into the life of a teenage football team in Belfast, as told by Ben Elton's book and lyrics and Andrew Lloyd Webber's music in *The Beautiful Game*, which has just opened at the Cambridge Theatre. Yearning for a time when they can live and play football in peace, they soon learn that to escape from bigotry and intolerance will take all the courage they can muster.

This month our cinemas will play *Billy Elliot*, a film about a young boy moving from boxing lessons to ballet classes in the local gym. We also have a film called *There's Only One Jimmy Grimble* about a Manchester school's football team and the attention it attracts from a local football scout. This plot also highlights the effect on the young players of both school bullies and of parents splitting up.

All these current productions have really hit home to me personally. In the forties I dreamed as a teenager of being Fred Astaire or Gene Kelly and I joined a dance class only to hang up my tap shoes when I found I also had to spend hours as a butterfly or snowflake. Years later I really hoped that *Fiddler On The Roof* would be an inspiration to Jewish aspirations for peace in Israel and the *West Side Story* help to resolve national intolerance of mixed marriages in countries such as Ireland.

But do these plays and films really reach home? We know that a dismally small number of party politicians ever take an interest in the arts. Equally we know that all too few of the thousands of sports spectators ever visit a theatre or cinema.

The annual Review of Football Finance by Deloitte & Touche showed that four million people attend league football matches in London compared with the 11.5 million attending West End theatres.

Further, the income from West End theatre ticket sales totalled £246 million in 1997 whereas gate receipts at league football was one-quarter of that sum (£60 million).

In the past, I have tried to interest ex-prisoners from Wandsworth (where I was once a visiting magistrate) in plays about crime and its effect on the community. Occasionally I met with success, even to the point when one ex-prisoner eventually became a stagehand in the West End.

But one really wonders whether the effort was worthwhile. Perhaps some people, from all levels of society, simply gravitate naturally to theatregoing just as others go fishing (and we do not subsidise worms to encourage more anglers).

Recently I have attempted to interest members of an under-16 football team, of which I have found myself to be chairman, in visiting stage productions. I warned them they were going to *Romeo and Juliet* set to music and they ended up at *West Side Story* in Woking.

Then they dreaded attending an up-to-date *Madame Butterfly*, but when they finally got to *Miss Saigon* at Drury Lane they enjoyed it. Their third visit was to see how ballet dancers are more virile than footballers (in *Fosse* which, like a football match, has not got a story). Some of them are now theatregoers, others are just bored and prefer to stay at home watching television.

I remain frustrated at any attempt to win over the young people who have sunk into a cesspit of indifference to any standards, both at school and at home where there is no encouragement by making available books, decent newspapers and magazines, or a chance ever to look at worthwhile television or listen to good radio programmes.

So will *Stones In His Pockets*, *Billy Elliot*, *There's Only One Jimmy Grimble* or *The Beautiful Game* do anything to change our lives or raise our standards?

Tourism and Theatre

This may seem a curious article unless you know that Tony has a long-standing holiday home on the island of Gozo, off Malta, in the Mediterranean. This isn't one of his strongest pieces, but I've included it as the issue of tourism and theatre is an important one in England, not least because the clichés associated with discussion of the subject are often raised in more general debate about the state of British theatre and, naturally, of London theatre in particular.

Tourism accounts for a sizeable portion of theatre receipts in London, and of the tourists who come to the West End, the majority are Americans, with the Japanese seemingly in second place – as anyone who has stood outside Her Majesty's Theatre and watched the coach-loads of Japanese arriving to see *The Phantom of the Opera* will agree.

On the other hand, the absence of Americans (after the first and second Gulf Wars, and at various points of international terrorism or instability) is a very convenient scapegoat for producers of shows that simply do not attract enough people because they can't cut the mustard.

Unlike the Mediterranean spots that Tony refers to in his article, London is not an unspoiled place of great natural beauty in danger of being changed for ever by the regular arrival of hordes of tourists or the creation of year-round resorts. On the contrary, London is a densely populated international city for whom foreign visitors are an essential ingredient. It is mass-market tourists who tend to descend on beaches: it is up market tourists who flock to the West End's theatres, restaurants and luxury hotels.

Even so, success can breed problems and irrevocable change. The London example that Tony gives is Covent Garden, which he feels is a victim of its success. The transformation of this area of central London from a wasteland when the old fruit and veg market (immortalised in *Pygmalion*) moved out, into a trendy and much-visited tourist trap (so much so that entry into the tube station is closed on many Saturdays due to unacceptably dangerous pressure of numbers), has indeed brought some unwelcome developments in its wake, like the loss of most of the older, more interesting and individual shops, auction houses and emporia, replaced by the inevitable 'fashionable' clothing stores. Long-standing theatrical establishments, like the Urdang Dance Academy have also moved out.

On the other hand, some improvements have been made: the boutiques, wine bars and restaurants that now fill the spaces where Eliza Doolittle and her friends plied their trade are far more interesting, convivial – and a lot less smelly – than the piles of fruit and veg (plus accompanying rodents) that used to occupy the market, while the Royal Ballet School has moved from West London into the heart of Covent Garden, right next to the Opera House. That building, too, has been completely and stunningly restored, thanks in part to American money, so there are plenty of benefits to tourism as well as drawbacks, and as long as theatre is (as it remains) one of the main tourist draws to London, then it will continue to benefit from foreign visitors.

PW

Tourism and Theatre

The Times of Malta, 23 March 2000

It was heartening to read the message made by Dr Michael Refalo, Parliamentary Secretary for Tourism, on World Tourism Day. It was wise on his part to emphasise the importance of tourism to the Island's economic well-being, but there are other important aspects to consider.

The scales of justice held by the blind goddess whose statue hangs over the high courts of the Old Bailey in London are a symbol of the balance of law and order, which judges and lawyers attempt to achieve.

Similarly, accountants' financial transactions are finalised in balance sheets whereby assets and liabilities are balanced. Throughout life, all our affairs need to be balanced and the most difficult achievement for any country is to have to balance its political, social, cultural and financial affairs.

Where there is an imbalance people suffer. To hold back a country's financial affairs produces hardship as one saw under the Czar's regime in Russia.

To advance too quickly, as with the same country's revolution, brings equal suffering and misery. The natural progression of civilisation is enormously difficult to bring about in a sensible and orderly way.

Malta, and in particular Gozo, are at such a turning point in their history and development. Malta's politicians and leading businessmen should take heed of the last quarter of a century's social development in many European countries and weigh in balance the assets and liabilities which have emerged from such development.

First Spain, then perhaps Portugal, Italy, ex-Yugoslavia and Greece have all been grappling with these problems in various stages.

They are countries which start with the advantages of great natural beauty, excellent warm weather and relatively low living costs – three enormous attractions for tourists, particularly from Germany, Scandinavia and the United Kingdom and, with increasing ease of international travel, from Canada, the United States and Australia.

It is impossible to deny that there should be a natural growth of tourism. As the world grows smaller with international travel becoming easier, passport and currency regulation becoming more sensible and artificial barriers of language and customs being broken down by education, one is forced to ask how one should define 'natural development'.

The citizens of an island like Gozo have a right to the benefits of modern civilisation – they should have the advantages of electricity (which such concomitant benefits as refrigeration), they should have better roads, schools, hospitals and the trappings of basic human rights.

But how is one to pay for them? How is one to balance the books of a government?

In Spain, they have been balancing the books by allowing uncontrolled development of large hotels and blocks of holiday apartments, with the accompanying shops and garages and pools, etc., along vast miles of seafronts of the tourist resorts.

Many now look like the tourist resorts in either the United States or the United Kingdom so that if a traveller woke up in one of them he would scarcely know which country he was in.

Thus, the tourists moved on to discover other unmolested spots further afield. And without a strong government and a civilised business community other countries have allowed themselves to sacrifice long-term benefits for short-term capital gain.

For what is left after the first decade or so of uncontrolled development?

The beautiful but possibly deprived little villages are replaced by ugly seaside developments which thrive like flowers opening up but then wilt and decay.

One is left with slums and crime of a kind a thousand times worse than in the poor but happy picturesque places they replaced.

Let us not be smug about this. Even communities with good intentions do not have the farsightedness to get it right.

In Britain when the Covent Garden fruit and vegetable market moved out of the centre of London it was planned to develop a market area around the Opera House with the 'cottage industries' that should be found in a cultural area.

Thus, boutiques and cafes were encouraged to open there, costumiers and button-makers servicing the theatre industry were encouraged to stay, bookshops and fringe music and theatre companies were invited to develop. All the same environment that New York encouraged to develop round the Lincoln Centre and Paris round the Pompidou Centre.

But the problem with arts and cultural centres is that they do thrive. They do bring into a community the ancillary business benefits of shops and restaurants and garages and the accoutrements of success.

One only has to experience the exciting life around any successful theatre or opera house or arts centre to see the rise in the whole standard of living, quality of life and, even more significantly, the higher land values in the surrounding district.

Hence, a fast food chain which attempted to buy into the Covent Garden area admitted that it was unlikely to meet with immediate success in such an up-market area but argued that being 'of Covent Garden' would be a good selling-point worldwide and that in any case their presence would help to down-market the area to their standards.

Thus, the Covent Garden area which a decade ago was becoming a haven for artists, writers, singers, actors, composers an designers has now become a down-market bazaar of Union Jack mugs and sleazy slogans on T-shirts - and the artists are priced out and driven away.

I have no answer as to how city authorities, let alone central governments, can deal with this problem. Too much artificial control can stunt the market and too much *laissez-faire* can kill the golden goose.

I have been working, as one of the Theatre Projects Consultants, on the new International Concert Hall in Athens. It is a far-sighted and supremely intelligent investment by the Greek government led by a visionary businessman, Christos Lambrakis.

But even then, I do not yet know what will be the eventual consequences to the whole environment of a thriving and successful concert hall playing to over 2,500 people over 300 nights a year.

Audiences flocking to a modern air-conditioned building playing popular concerts and recitals of symphonic music, dance and opera with international orchestras and artistes will require supporting computerised box offices, car parking facilities, road access, restaurants and bars, hotels and garages.

Many of these assets are already available or are being planned. But the long term effect of such developments in the area are difficult to assess.

Similarly, the primitive charm of a delightful island like Gozo has started to be developed in the past decade bringing with it a higher standard of living to many inhabitants.

One looks across Gozo at the towering outline of the wonderful church at Xewkija and realises that it looks like what St Paul's Cathedral looked to Canaletto.

But does Gozo want eventually to see buildings dwarf their churches as they do in London? And any plans to further develop resorts like Marsalforn and Xlendi will easily destroy the assets that Gozo possesses.

These assets are not only the tangible ones of scenery, sea and sun but the wonderful family life which is prevalent there and which is already lost to so many so-called civilised communities.

Allowing mobile snack bars at Ramla Bay or a hotel to be built at Xlendi may be a well-argued short-term asset, but the long-term liabilities are incalculable.

It is only then that the accountants will find that the balance sheet no longer balances and that the scales of justice are tipped against the entire population.

5 AUDIENCE REACTION

The following two articles, written in the first few years of the 21st century, have more recently been reflected in an article in *The Times* by a senior arts journalist, Ian Johns, in which he writes that audiences seem to be harking back to a late eighteenth and early nineteenth century tradition of noisy interaction between audience and actor – even if this is only (usually) manifested at curtain calls, with audiences giving sporadic standing ovations and actors responding by applauding their applauders.

The fact remains that London audiences are less vociferous than New York ones, and theatre audiences far less so than ballet or opera-goers. The anecdotes that Tony quotes about exchanges between Gallery First-Nighters and actors are real but read as if they come from a far-distant age rather than well within living memory. As anecdotes they sound (although undoubtedly reliable) almost too good to be true. Anyone who has ever seen an actor stumble over a line, let alone forget one, or be thrown by an unexpected noise from the stalls (usually late-comers) will find the idea of spontaneously witty exchanges between performers and hecklers hard to believe.

Yet the fact remains that they took place, and in an age where audience reaction was more immediate and more vocal, actors had to be more on their toes. It is also the ace, of course, that by and large it was the poorer actors who received most audible comment, so they were presumably used to (if not inured to) getting feedback from their customers, and therefore both less surprised and more able to react when it happened.

Tony quotes the case of Coward's *Sirocco* in the 1920s, as a prime example of an audience letting their displeasure known; in fact the fracas was even worse than he mentions. When Ivor had his big romantic scene with his leading lady, Frances Doble, disgruntled audience members made loud kissing noises on the backs of their hands. Coward, ushering Miss Doble forward for an extra bow at curtain call, despite the jeers and catcalls, was greeted with the ironic cry of "Hide behind a woman, would you?" at which point Miss Doble, who had broken down in hysterics, went onto auto pilot and gave her prepared curtain call speech: "Ladies and gentlemen," she stammered, tears coursing down her face as the boos and hisses mounted in volume, "tonight is the happiest night of my life!"

One of the main attractions of the Gallery First-Nighters Club, referred to in these articles, was the sense of community that these theatre-goers enjoyed. At a time when theatre-going was more a part of everyday life for some people (admittedly the determined few) and in an age when the cost of theatre-going was, relatively, far cheaper, there was a real atmosphere of comradeship, of shared enjoyment as well as occasional expressions of displeasure, and a sense, too, of ownership of theatres and plays. When an audience knows a play (especially Shakespeare) like the back of its hand, and is equally familiar with a theatre building and with many of the actors on stage, the old cliché about the audience being an essential part of a play, and of the actors owing them tribute for their professional success, has a real ring of truth about it.

Today's audiences are less vocal, not because they are more polite but because, in a sense, they are often less committed. Given the cost of London theatre-going in particular, a trip to the theatre is a major event, and customers want desperately to enjoy themselves. To boo, let alone heckle, would be an admission that they have been short-changed, that they have spent money on a spectacle that they have not enjoyed. This is more than they can bear, so they remain silent. Unless, to be fair, they are at the opera, but then opera directors are more inclined than theatre ones to foist atrociously pretentious rubbish on long-suffering and high-paying audiences. I can still remember the jeers, boos and catcalls that greeted English National Opera's *Mazeppa* at the Coliseum in the mid 1980s, when an opera about a Cossack was represented on stage by chainsaw-wielding Mafiosi splattering the stage with fake blood.

The obverse of this, the lack of standing ovations, is more a cultural difference than one of historical period: New Yorkers readily leap to their feet, especially for musicals, in a way that British audiences are reluctant to do. Standing ovations still count as untoward displays of emotion, and, though we live in a post-Diana age, the majority of people, unless they have been whipped up by a rock opera like the appropriately-named *We Will Rock You*, the Rod Stewart musical *Tonight's The Night* or the invariably feel-good phenomenon that is *Mamma Mia!*, prefer to remain resolutely in their seats.

There remains, then, a delicate balance (as Edward Albee might have put it) between a very English desire not to make a fuss, plus a civilised intention to let actors and directors do their stuff under the most propitious circumstances, and, on the other hand, a natural and indeed admirable refusal to put up with shoddy sets, staging and performance when paying through the nose, sitting in seats designed for Victorian midgets and having faced a nightmare scrum for

a much-needed drink in the interval. This is clearly an issue that will continue to crop up as long as plays are performed.
PW

Audience Reaction

The Stage, 30 March 2000

One of the London theatre scene's losses has been the disappearance of Gallery First-Nighters, which were a moderating influence on works being produced.

Along with professional critics, they were a force to be reckoned with because their cheers or boos were frequently reported as a balance to what reviews were telling the public.

Often led by the powerful voice of Sophie, a theatregoer from London's East End, the voices from the gods resounded through theatres on first nights.

Crowds had queued for their gallery places, usually putting down stools for sixpence in an orderly line during the day until the doors to these unreserved seats opened half-an-hour before the performance. Seating was usually on long benches, now replaced by tip-up seats costing between 40 and 80 times the 1946 price.

Actors were generally fearful of the reaction from the gallery, but admitted that an occasional booing was worth the warmth of the cheering on other occasions. The hard-working, theatre-mad people in the gods were also a balance against the wealthy, well-dressed investors and friends of the cast who sat in the stalls and politely received what was on the stage.

There was also the formality of the Gallery First-Nighters Club. Leslie Bloom served as its president for 21 years, and its regular dinners were graced by speeches from leading actors, who were often presented with special awards.

Galleryites rarely interrupt a performance. I can only remember one occasion, on which they shouted "speak up" to an aged Lilian Braithwaite when she appeared with Ralph Richardson in his 1948 production of *Royal Circle*.

Would that the voices from the gods have been at *The Real Thing* at the Albery, when shouts from the stalls pleaded "speak up", followed by a round of applause from frustrated playgoers.

The production's stars, Stephen Dillane and Jennifer Ehle, blamed the move from the 251 seat Donmar Warehouse to the 879 seat Albery.

But this beautiful venue, which was built for Charles Wyndham, has superb acoustics and has housed hundreds of productions without such problems over the sound of actors' voices.

Too many current stars have had no proper professional voice training, and have spent so much time in television and films that they cannot adapt from one live venue to another.

But the cast of Trevor Nunn's recent revival of The *Merchant of Venice* has managed it, successfully moving from the 200 seat Cottesloe to the 1,160 seat Olivier, where even a whisper from trained actors can be heard at the back of the circle.

It was amusing to hear Dillane say the next day: "That's never happened to me, though I'm aware I am sometimes inaudible. We may just give up on the whole thing, stand at the front, smile and shout".

If that is what present-day acting is about, bring back the Gallery First-Nighters, We shall see what happens when this production moves to the Belasco Theatre in New York, which has around 100 more seats than the Albery.

I do not deny that audiences have become acclimatised to the louder sounds of television and cinema. Attention spans have also deteriorated, with modern entertainment providing short, two-minute scenes which can be watched passively from an armchair.

But apart from actors, what are directors, producers, set designers and lighting and sound technicians doing about these matters of audibility?

Do they ever sit in the cheapest seats or those with restricted views to ascertain whether playgoers are getting their money's worth?

What might have been accepted in 1946 from a seat costing ten pence might not be so pleasing at the current £15.

To Boo Or Not To Boo

The Stage, 22 November 2001

Recently, the media has drawn attention to a minority of opera audiences who have chosen to boo a production and a suggestion has been made that a slip in the programme could well canvas patrons as to whether a production has helped or hindered their appreciation of the work in question. Jonathan Miller was once assailed by an opera-goer after his production of *Rigoletto*, to say "you have ruined Verdi's opera", to which he replied "Madam, I may have ruined your night at *Rigoletto*, but Verdi's opera remains intact for all time".

With the demise of the Gallery First-Nighters Club, or perhaps just the replacement of the galleries' bench seats with tip-up seats at twenty times the price, the response by boos or cheers of first-nighters to a play appears to have become muted and routine. It was always a matter of argument as to whether booing was ethical in that usually the cast bore the brunt of an unfavourable reaction rather than the playwright or director. Usually at opera first nights separate curtain calls are given to the cast, the director, the designer et al, so the audience can direct their appreciation or otherwise to the specific quarter. However, at some first nights a dramatist has been prepared to shoulder the brunt of jeers. At the end of a dismal play, *Ambassador Extraordinary* by William Douglas Home, directed by Sir Cedric Hardwicke, at the Aldwych in 1948 the dramatist came on stage to face the barrage of jeers and announced "The time will come when you will have to listen to what this play tells you," to which Sophie (the indefatigable gallery first-nighter) shouted "Rubbish, young man". William Douglas Home looked up and said "I don't mind being heckled, Sophie," and got her response: "You are not being heckled, you are being judged!"

On rare occasions, a play was interrupted during a performance that often caused fights outside the theatre after a first night. A dreadful play, *All The Year Round*, by Neville Croft at the Duke of York's Theatre in 1950 came in for heckling during the first night performance and many theatregoers remonstrated with the gallery-goers to the effect that if a cast came forward at the curtain call to receive cheers or boos the reaction was legitimate criticism, but to interrupt a play was unfair to the production and disturbing to the playgoers.

On one occasion, Emile Little knew he had a flop on his hands and was determined to avoid confrontation with the gallery, so he opened his show on a

Wednesday matinee at the Duke of York's Theatre and immediately closed it before the evening performance, knowing that the Gallery First-Nighters nearly all worked and could not attend a mid-week matinee. Many regulars remained frustrated forever at having missed this one performance in their entire career of theatregoing.

The only time I found an interruption of a play was possibly justified was at the first night of *Royal Circle* at Wyndham's Theatre in 1948 with Dame Lilian Braithwaite and Sir Ralph Richardson, when Sophie shouted out towards the end of their first act "Speak up, Sir Ralph!" and he certainly did so in the next act; no doubt because he was also the director!

On many occasions the Gallery First-Nighters withheld any booing until they found whether the stalls were giving polite applause which they considered unjustified and the booing then started at the second or third curtain call. Of course, an experienced company manager would seek to know the temperature of a first-night audience in the interval from the House Manager and would then arrange with the stage manager for one quick curtain and then go into 'house lights'. This often stifled any booing and ensured that any bad reaction would not be reported in the press the next morning. Nothing was worse than an inexperienced stage manager's milking the curtain calls unjustifiably; and equally stifling a cheering audience by cutting them short would also prove irritating. There was certainly an art in such decisions.

Most actors accepted that it was worth the ghastly nights they were booed for the memorable glory of the cheers after a success and it was considered healthy for theatre generally, not just to get polite applause at the end of every production. The practice of booing rarely spread to American audiences and dismal first nights on Broadway are greeted by the sound of seats being vacated as the audience slips out during the last act so that the cast at a failure finds a near-empty theatre when they come to take their curtain call.

Even some of our most successful and glamorous theatrical figures have been involved in disastrous curtain calls. One remembers the successes – Ivor Novello's *Glamorous Night*, *The Dancing Years* and *King's Rhapsody*, or Noel Coward's *Cavalcade*, *Blithe Spirit* and *Private Lives*, just as we remember Cameron Mackintosh's successes with *Cats*, *The Phantom of the Opera* and *Les Mis*. But all of these impressively creative figures had their box office failures – in the case of Cameron Mackintosh the fate of *Café Puccini*, *Moby Dick* and *Martin Guerre* was nothing compared to those of Novello and Coward.

Noel Coward recorded in his autobiography that during the first performance of his comedy *Home Chat* in 1927 at the Duke of York's he realised that the gallery was growing restless so at the curtain he dashed from his box to the stage as he felt that it was unfair for the actors to bear the brunt of a bad reception. The moment he appeared the booing from the gallery and the pit grew louder and a voice from the pit yelled "Rotten!" and one from the gallery "we expected a better play" whereupon Coward snapped back that he expected better manners and the final curtain fell amid considerable tumult.

Later in 1927, Coward's next play, *Sirocco*, starred Ivor Novello, whose film fans jammed into the gallery at Daly's Theatre and gave him a big reception on his entrance. But the evening was a disaster with the gallery and pit yelling through the last act while the stalls shushed. Basil Dean, who produced the play, normally never attended his first nights. However, although he had spent the evening dining somewhere, he turned up at the end conceivably mistaking the boos for cheers and stood in the prompt corner smiling and ringing the curtain up and down. Coward disillusioned him and walked on to the stage to shake hands with Ivor, which increased the booing ten fold. It was recorded that it was one of the angriest uproars ever heard in a theatre.

Eighteen months later the gallery at His Majesty's was cheering *Bitter Sweet*; *Sirocco* was forgiven if not forgotten. One cannot help thinking that the theatre scene was livelier in those days and when we got rid of the galleries and the pits we lost an intrinsic element of the drama and music scene.

6 THEATRE ISSUES

Theatre – A Millennium Survey

This article begins and ends with a quote from Oscar Hammerstein:

> *Oh, the theatre is dying, the theatre is dying,*
> *The theatre is practically dead.*

And Tony goes on to refute that statement, referring to the way that theatre has reinvented itself through the ages, and to the impossibility of predicting which plays or playwrights will be discarded after their initial appearance (fashionable or otherwise) and which will be treasured, or rediscovered and promoted, long after initially more popular and commercial writers and productions have disappeared into oblivion.

As he says, theatre had its origins in medieval mystery plays, though of course there was a great body of work, extant if not performed, dating from the days of Ancient Greece.

The real explosion of drama came in Elizabethan times, when, as he mentions, along with the well-known open air theatres (brilliantly recreated today on Bankside, thanks to the Globe) was the less well-known indoor theatre of Blackfriars, where some of Shakespeare's later plays (including *The Tempest*) were performed.

One of the major developments that is not mentioned in the millennium article is the decision (implemented by Charles II on his Restoration in 1660) to have women play female roles on stage. Until the popular film *Shakespeare in Love* brought it to the wider public's attention, it was a little-known fact that Shakespeare, Marlowe, and other pre-Restoration playwrights wrote all their great female parts for teenage boys, it being considered indecent for women to appear on stage. This extraordinary fact (to our minds) was itself well represented on stage by Nicholas Wright's *Cressida*, a play centred on a theatre company in the 1630s, where an older actor (Sir Michael Gambon) was in charge of a group of young men, many of whom played female parts – hence the play's title.

It is impossible to cover every aspect of a thousand years of theatre history in a book, let alone an article, and some aspects, like the extraordinary propensity of London theatres to burn to the ground (especially Drury Lane, ruining the playwright and theatre owner Richard Brinsley Sheridan in the process), don't get a mention. What is clear, however, is the ability of theatre to reinvent itself, to meet the cultural and commercial needs of each age, and to provide both an entertainment for, and mirror to, society.

It was the power of theatre to move audiences and to change the way they saw the world that led to the censorship to which Tony refers, and if these days the providers of financial support are governments and local councils rather than Kings and aristocrats, then so be it, so long as theatre continues to flourish and develop in the new millennium as it did in the previous one.
PW

Oscar Hammerstein wrote, in *Me and Juliet:*

Oh, the theatre is dying, the theatre is dying,
The theatre is practically dead.

Well, some might say it has been dying for the past 2,000 years but happily I am only looking back over my diaries for the past millennium. The front page of *The Stage* states that it was established in 1880, but does not reveal that the stage in its wider sense was disestablished by the church in the previous millennium together with the destruction of all theatres, so we were left with small groups of medieval minstrels travelling from village to village.

By 1100 the church itself had brought drama back into existence and Christmas and Easter stories were developed so successfully that performances later moved out of churches and into the open air.

These mystery and miracle plays gave way to morality plays and then to interludes, short dramatic pieces played at court and country houses, between the endless courses of early Tudor banquets. Some of the best interludes were written by John Heywood, one of the first English dramatic writers.

The colourful and rowdy inn-yard audiences were continually being driven out of the City of London by prosperous merchants, so that James Burbage, father of Richard and a stage-struck joiner and actor who was also a property developer of genius, took a lease of land in Shoreditch and built the world's first public-private enterprise theatre, The Theatre.

The Theatre was a wooden building, open to the skies, seating 3,000 people and was swiftly followed by another theatre nearby called The Curtain. Admission was one penny, with another penny for a seat on a bench and a third penny for a better seat on the stands.

Thus the great age of British drama began with John Lyly, Christopher Marlowe, whose *Tamburlaine the Great* delighted audiences at The Theatre where a call-boy and hack writer started work – William Shakespeare had arrived in 1586.

By 1600 it was estimated that one Londoner in eight went to the theatre once a week and, by then, Burbage had built the Blackfriars Theatre, the first of the public indoor venues where productions of Shakespeare's plays could be given in winter, when the weather made productions impossible in the huge, open wooden O.

Within 40 years all the great plays of British drama were written by Shakespeare and Marlowe and by Ben Jonson, Heywood, John Webster, Philip Massinger and Francis Beaumont and John Fletcher. However, in 1642 Parliament banned stage plays and theatres were all closed.

British drama then came to life again with Restoration theatre, a different style, being often witty, gay, artificial and amoral, which gave rise to Restoration Comedy. More spectacular productions emerged, as did pantomime and *The Beggar's Opera* by John Gay.

Thus we moved into the 1700s with the building of the first provincial theatres at Bath (1705), Bristol (1729) and Ipswich (1736), to house comedies by William Wycherley, William Congreve and John Vanbrugh.

But once again, politicians worried about the frank farces which mocked them, so in 1737 Robert Walpole put theatres under strict control, banned touring companies and imposed censorship on all new plays, which had to be read and licensed by the Lord Chamberlain.

Nevertheless, theatre continued to progress in the 18th century due largely to the emergence of David Garrick, an immediate success as an actor, who shook British theatre out of its old habits. As a central figure of artistic authority Garrick changed the mannered and declamatory style of acting into something more realistic.

As manager of Drury Lane Theatre he instituted such reforms as requiring actors to rehearse and have some grasp of their lines. He also introduced improved lighting and more elaborate scenery.

However, during these hundred years only two great playwrights and their plays emerged from hundreds of new plays and writers who were around. Oliver Goldsmith with *She Stoops To Conquer* and Richard Brinsley Sheridan with *The School for Scandal*, both masterpieces of the Comedy of Manners.

In the early 1800s, theatre buildings moved to keep pace with the increasing influence of the middle classes. Gas lighting was introduced in 1817, the front pit was removed to the back so orchestra stalls could be introduced at higher prices in 1820 and the first dress circle was so named in 1822. But, by 1870, drama was on the wane again; politicians ensured that the Lord Chamberlain acquired tighter powers of censorship and Matthew Arnold cried: "We have no drama at all."

A new theatrical influence then emerged in the form of the actor-manager who leased and often owned a theatre, hired and fired the cast, chose the repertoire, took the star role and often rewrote the script to ensure his performance dominated. One of the greatest of these actor-managers was Henry Irving, who became the first actor to be knighted.

Once again, out of this mediocrity, rose one comedy playwright of genius, Oscar Wilde, and plays of ideas started to emerge from writers such as Henry Arthur Jones, Arthur Wing Pinero, T W Robertson and George Bernard Shaw. *Mrs Warren's Profession* was written in 1893 but not publicly performed in Britain until 1920 because of the Lord Chamberlain's censorship. None of Shaw's plays were performed in public until he was over 40, for such were the fears of party politicians.

The era of the actor-managers ended with the First World War, by which time property prices were so high that landlords became distinct from the producers of plays who, in turn, engaged directors.

There was a body of opinion that held that theatre was dying yet again between the two world wars, this time due to the phenomenal popularity of the cinema. In turn, after the Second World War, filmgoers were lured away from the theatre to the convenience of television.

Modern theatre needs government subsidy to keep it alive, in the same way that the mystery plays relied on the support of the church and the Elizabethan theatre flourished under royal patronage.

Thus in 1939 the Council for the Encouragement of the Arts was established to keep the arts alive during the war, which led to the foundation of the Arts Council of Great Britain in 1946.

Not only did the Arts Council encourage the development of some 40 regional theatre companies but also, through its Housing the Arts plans (foreshadowing the National Lottery) it ensured the building or redevelopment of new theatres all over Scotland, Wales and the English regions to house existing companies.

One of the most important companies to get financial support from the Arts Council was the English Stage Company. The idea for this creative venture emanated from a conversation between Ronald Duncan and Oscar Lewenstein in 1953 and within a year the company was producing at the Royal Court under the direction of George Devine. This was to change the face of British theatre for the second half of the 20th century, starting with John Osborne's *Look Back In Anger*, which suffered at the hands of the Lord Chamberlain who insisted on cuts being made.

Sadly, the prodigious efforts required to maintain the successful vision of the English Stage Company led to the deaths of George Devine, Neville Blond and Robin Fox. The remaining board members and the theatre building, with continuing Arts Council subsidy, were left searching for a new policy, which was one of the dangers of institutionalisation.

One of the most rewarding decisions I ever made was to help launch the New Watergate Theatre Club at the Comedy Theatre so it could produce *A View From the Bridge*, *Cat on a Hot Tin Roof*, and *Tea and Sympathy*. Although it had not set out to influence a change in the law, such action undoubtedly led to the Theatres Act of 1968, which abolished the Lord Chamberlain's power of censorship.

The resulting freedom for dramatists, together with the growing influence of the national and regional theatres under the aegis of the Arts Council, led to greater unease from all political parties.

It appeared as if the theatre was still disturbing politicians, having survived 2,000 years of suppression, poverty, excommunication and creative malnutrition, for it could still represent the substance of truth and faith. As a result there came about the systematic destruction of a system which was the envy of the world.

The Arts Council of Great Britain was divided into three councils (one each for England, Scotland and Wales) and the Arts Council devolved into its ten Regional Arts Associations. Consequently, there is no longer any one forceful voice to save the theatre from dying, and many of the theatres built or restored with Housing the Arts funds have since closed for lack of revenue funding.

Unfortunately, space dictates that other elements of the theatre such as British music hall and operetta from Noel Coward and Ivor Novello to Andrew Lloyd Webber, the great impact of European playwrights from Molière to Henrik Ibsen and the American theatre from Clifford Odets to its musicals can only be alluded to here.

This brief summary also shows how difficult it can be to assess the importance of contemporary playwrights. Who would have thought that the enormous West End successes of plays by T S Eliot and Christopher Fry would now largely be forgotten some 40 years later or that some of the apparently superficial plays by Terence Rattigan and Coward are now moving into our classical repertoire?

Perhaps the last word could be given to Cameron Mackintosh if he were prepared to revive *Me and Juliet*, which is where we began:

> *Oh, the theatre is dying, the theatre is dying,*
> *The theatre is practically dead.*

Has Broadway More Buzz?

The main point about the contrast between London and New York that Tony makes in this 1989 article is that New York has a wider variety of theatres which are open at a variety of times, and that theatre is taken more seriously in the States.

In many ways this is still true. The first few years of the 21st century have seen a real sense of malaise in the West End, with numerous articles and comments from leading theatre producers, critics and journalists despairing over the physical state of the West End, its uncomfortable seats, expensive drinks, rubbish-strewn streets, dark theatres and lack of really exciting new plays.

Despite the fact that far more people attend theatres each weekend than go to football matches, theatre hardly ever gets mentioned on the news – unless a high-profile actor dies – and the very few theatre events that are televised (The Olivier Awards, the Evening Standard Drama Awards) go out late at night, never at prime time.

There is, still, a real sense of pride in its theatre in New York, in a way that simply doesn't exist in London, where the attitude to the theatre is either *blasé* or smug – "It's the best in the world, innit?" Theatre is not only taken more seriously in New York, it is also enjoyed more. So often one hears from people, whether actors or theatregoers, that in New York audiences actually seem to want to *enjoy* a performance, that you can sense them willing the performers to succeed. In London that simply isn't the case, with the exception of some of the jollier musicals, where people already know the tunes and expect to have a good time – as at *Mamma Mia!* for example.

This desire for, and general atmosphere of, enjoyment is marked by the different approach towards standing ovations. London audiences still consider these to be rather too emotional to be good form, whereas in New York they love to show their appreciation by standing to applaud – in straight plays as well as musicals. In London, a standing ovation may happen at a musical but is incredibly rare at a play.

To be fair to the West End, London's theatres are prettier and more historic than most of those in New York, and any night of the week you can also find a staggering array of plays and musicals being performed in fringe venues from the centre to the outskirts of town in addition to the selection presented in the West End, and it's also true that first nights have a certain flavour to them, too.

However, far fewer people dress up to go to the theatre in the West End than they do on Broadway (and they only ever appear in black tie at a Royal Gala).

Only opera (and, to a degree, ballet) audiences dress with any sense of verve or style in London. This inevitably means that there is less of a sense of occasion about theatregoing in London than in New York and, therefore, less of a buzz. We've got the theatres, playwrights and actors in London – we just need to make up our minds to *enjoy* them more.

PW

Has Broadway More Buzz?

The Stage, 2 November 1989

Earlier this year, when I visited New York, I again fell to wondering what makes Broadway theatregoing quite so exciting when its actual creativity is so far short of what we are privileged to see in London. Well, first and foremost, the media there give it more prominence than is given to sport whereas in Britain perhaps the legacy of Lords Reith and Beaverbrook lingers on with the thought that 'sport is a healthy past-time for the masses' and 'we don't want to encourage the general population to think'.

Hence, the BBC1 television news gave two and a half minutes at 9.30p.m. on a Saturday evening to a soccer game at Wimbledon attended by 6,000 people – little more than go to the two Saturday performances at Drury Lane Theatre. The West End theatres attract well over 250,000 people a week (with over a quarter of a million people visiting regional theatres each week) and get very little news coverage at all except when an Andrew Lloyd Webber musical opens or a Laurence Olivier dies. But every hour the news report is followed by '…and now sport', when we hear about the women's bob-sleigh team in Finland and the men's marbles championship in Tasmania. I live in hope of hearing '…and now the arts and entertainment', but this is always relegated to a late Sunday-night ghetto-ised programme.

In New York I was surprised to find myself attending the *Kathy and I* show at 3p.m. on a Sunday and the first night of *Born Yesterday* that evening! The theatre attorney who sat next to me pointed out the importance of planning a first-night on a Sunday. "Newspaper critics are no longer as influential as they were. New productions now rely heavily on the television critics and everyone, but everyone, tunes into television for the critical reviews after 10.p.m. and, most particularly, everyone is watching these on a Sunday night". Hence the masses of television cameras outside the 46th Street Theatre filming the crowds entering. At the final curtain, the cameras rushed in to film the reception and the curtain speech by Ed Asner calling up Garson Kanin from the audience. The flowers and the tears were all there which no doubt resulted in future audiences responding to 'the human factor' of show business which British television ignores, choosing instead to be competitive with the theatre it feeds off.

Also sitting with me at that first night was Joy Franz who was appearing the rest of the week in Sondheim's *Into The Woods* and who last night appeared in London in his *Company*. She was delighted to be able to go to another production on her night off – another enormous asset for the availability of theatres seven days a week in New York.

We all marched down Whitehall all those years ago to support the Sunday Observance Bill amendments and yet we have still not taken advantage of that success. It is increasingly essential that all arts and entertainment organisations are available when required by the public any day of the week or any hour of the day. Let us hope that the pioneering work achieved by *Siegfried Sassoon* at the Apollo, *Lennon* at the Astoria, *The Two Ronnies* at the Palladium and *Woman in Black* at the Strand, all of which played on Sundays, can lead to the more flexible policy achieved in New York. However, until a reasonable number of theatres adopt this flexibility it will require increased advertising expenditure to promote it. It will also require dedication to a policy of gearing standard rates of pay to a standard working week whenever it is worked. The increased income from providing the public with increased availability of theatres will provide the higher base rates long since justified instead of artificial 'overtime'.

I have written about the excitement of Broadway but its lack of creativity. This is illustrated in the success of the 1980 New York season comprising *Phantom, Cats, Les Misérables, Me and My Girl, Lettice and Lovage, Shirley Valentine, Run For Your Wife, Lend Me A Tenor, When I Was A Young Girl I Used to Scream And Shout*, and *Single Spies*.

However, the London theatre scene is not all that conducive to creative work. When I arrived in London in the forties there was a wonderful selection of Theatre Clubs – the Boltons, the New Lindsey, the Watergate, the Q, the Arts, the Gateway, the Embassy, Unity, the Mercury, the Torch, the Actor's, the Gate, the Chanticleer, the Tavistock, Hampstead, the Mercury, the Irving and others...

There were also the most useful suburban theatres like Kingston Empire, the Granville Walham Green, the King's Hammersmith and others. These were later followed by the fringe theatre companies, fostered by the Arts Council, Belt and Braces, Clown Cavalcade, Common Stock, Eastend Abbreviated Soapbox and so on.

The theatre needs this sort of mosaic. Companies like the National need the Cottesloe, the Royal Shakespeare needs the Pit, the Swan needs the Other Place and the West End needs not just the Donmar. There are nearly 40 theatres sitting on prime West End sites, open to the public some 24 hours per week. It behoves theatre landlords and West End producers to encourage their spaces to be used by small creative companies working at lunchtimes or late nights, filling the centre of our capital with rehearsed readings, new work, whatever...the waste of talent is shocking and all it needs is some encouragement and imagination from lively managements who control the venues. There are two new Rogers on the scene, Roger Filer (Stoll Moss) and Roger Wingate (Maybox), who, between them, are now responsible for the majority of West End theatres, and maybe these two lively minds will set new standards and open new horizons.

What's the Future for the RSC?

The Stage, 21 June 2001

Adrian Noble certainly has guts. He also has vision and integrity. But whether one is fully supportive or furiously critical of his plans for the future of the Royal Shakespeare Company, there are questions one has to ask.

When I was at the Arts Council I often suggested to my colleagues in the drama department that my finance officers could more easily asses subsidies if the drama officers were to divide the subsidised companies into those that provided a service to a region, being based in, say, Ipswich or Canterbury, Exeter or York, and those committed to producing new drama or new ways of producing old drama like, say, the English Stage Company, the Mermaid or the Royal Exchange Company.

The two national companies, the National and the Royal Shakespeare Company, each had their own ethos as agreed by the Arts Council and this straddled both commitments – that to their theatres and that to the development of drama production of the highest calibre.

It will, therefore, be interesting to learn what will be the basis of Noble's redevelopment proposals to be put to the Arts Council in September for future funding.

Following the closure of *The Secret Garden*, his present admirable thoughts are to present shorter runs with flexible contracts in a variety of working spaces. The exigencies which have led him to this thinking are exactly those which have dictated the policies of all our leading producers.

Duncan Weldon, Michael Codron and Michael Redington have all had their visions curtailed by actors who do not wish to sign contracts for more than three months and by directors who want to stage a production in a theatre best suited to the play although economically disastrous for their investors.

Michael Billington has asked what will give the new RSC its identity? No doubt the Arts Council will go on to ask how this identity will differ from any other producer or will they be all be asking for a modest £1 million subsidy each year.

Why not for, say, Thelma Holt, whose numerous productions have reflected her identity when you start to compile a few of them such as *Three Sisters* and *Orpheus Descending*, both with Vanessa Redgrave, *A Doll's House*, with Alan Rickman and Janet McTeer, *The Merchant of Venice*, with Dustin Hoffman, *King Lear*, with Nigel Hawthorne and her recent *Semi-Monde*, featuring a cast of 28?

Or why not Bill Kenwright's policy which has included *A Long Day's Journey Into Night*, *Waiting For Godot*, *Medea* with Diana Rigg, *Kafka's Dick* and *A Streetcar Named Desire* with Jessica Lange?

Then there is Robert Fox with Martin Sherman's *A Madhouse in Goa* and *When She Danced*, both with Vanessa Redgrave, *Three Tall Women* by Edward Albee, *Interpreters* by Ronald Harwood and *Lettice and Lovage* by Peter Shaffer, all three with Maggie Smith, *The Seagull* with Jonathan Pryce, *Another Country* by Julian Mitchell and *Vita and Virginia* by Eileen Atkins.

All our independent producers are ideas-led rather than formulaic, which is no doubt why Peter Hall finally left both the RSC and the NT to form his own unsubsidised company.

It is, perhaps, sad that fewer producers, directors, designers, actors and technicians want to work for our great artistic institutions, whether in the drama, music, opera or dance worlds.

Indeed, it is a great challenge and particularly restricting to have to service a particular building and a special audience whether it is in Liverpool or Covent Garden.

This is now a national problem for the British arts scene which has become so fragmented in the past decades that we no longer have the shrewd experience required by those who will have to resolve this matter.

The first European Conference of the International Society of Performing Arts Administration held in Prague proved to be both unique and exciting.

With the title The Arts and The New Europe it was most moving to be able to discus arts issues arising from the recent momentous changes in Central Europe in one of the cities which was at the centre of major political upheaval. The Society (ISPAA) is, of course, non-political in every sense of the phrase, but it would have been impossible for arts administrators from Central and Western Europe to meet and explore common concerns without some reference to the financial and administrative consequences resulting from major changes in the way certain people choose to be governed.

The conference opened with a splendid buffet hosted by the Ministry of Culture in the Knight's Hall of the Palace Waldstein where Richard Pulford, President of ISPAA and General Director (Administration) of the South Bank Centre in London, introduced Milan Udhe, the Minister of Culture of the Czechoslovak Republic since June 1990. Milan Udhe is a Doctor of Czech literature and a leading author of theatre, radio and television plays as well as being an active literary critic and writer of essays.

The minister welcomed the conference to Prague as a significant demonstration that Czechoslovakia has at last entered into Europe. He emphasised the great difficulties in moving the arts into a free market economy after the state had administered them for over 40 years. Whenever the state finances the arts fully there are problems of the state judging for itself what is the right art and how it should be served to the people. Further, there was great suspicion of those arts which were entertaining since it was considered that the arts should educate. In such an environment the artists themselves put up with the difficulties and gave in to state control.

After the first weeks of the Czechoslovakian revolution in 1989, the days of confusion were changed for one having to return to ordinary days of work and, in so doing, the only way was to back a market economy. There were then warnings from artists who had been living well under the previous regime that the market economy would lead to a decline in Czechoslovak culture.

Milan Udhe explained that he had always been a strong supporter of freedom being the only basis of artistic success and that the free market economy can only bring an improvement to the disastrous standards of creativity before the revolution.

However, the minister was concerned that there was no experience in Czechoslovakia of the market economy and such a conference could only assist in offering guidelines for the future. These were the reasons for his particularly warm welcome to delegates from 22 countries across the world.

I was privileged to discuss some issues with Milan Udhe, through an interpreter, and he expressed interest in our observations on their current difficulties in moving from a situation of state-controlled arts activities to one governed by a free market.

On the first full day of work the conference heard from Peter Sarah of the Contemporary Dance Trust in London who emphasised that arts administrators from Western Europe, from North America and from Central Europe all have much to learn from one another. His talk on 'Constructive Approaches to Central Europe' reminded everyone that creative artists needed the support of creative administrators. Future historians will depend on the artistic work to learn about current times and not on who is in a political post. It is, therefore, essential to allow the public the widest possible choice both in mainstream work and the new and dissident since today's fringe activities are tomorrow's market leaders.

Peter Sarah explained that, whilst sport depends on competition, the arts depend on cooperation and it was essential for arts administrators to have wide freedom to exchange experiences and assist each other through organisations such as ISPAA, the Council of Europe, UNESCO, the Informal European Theatre Meetings, the European Commission, the European Cultural Foundation and all Government Agencies.

Peter Sarah's plenary session was discussed by four groups, led by Hilde Teuchies of the Informal European Theatre Meeting in Brussels, John Elsom of the International Association of Theatre Critics, Michael Tearle from St David's Hall, Cardiff, and Rudolf Wolfensberger who is the Secretary-General of the Association for the Performing Arts in Amsterdam. John Elsom particularly highlighted the current complexities of the situation in countries such as Hungary, Poland and Czechoslovakia where audiences, not unlike those in Western Europe and North America, are staying in front of their television sets.

The second plenary session was led by Tom Harris speaking on New Management and Sponsorship ion the New Europe. This session was chaired by Arnold Breman, the President-elect of ISPAA and one of the leading artistic directors in North America. It was generally agreed that sponsorship was almost at its peak in North America and Western Europe, particularly in the light of the economic recession and the effects of the Gulf War. Delegates from Central Europe emphasised the great difficulties of raising any sponsorship in their countries and we were warned of its fickle nature if arts organisations were looking for a consistent basis of income to replace declining support from central government subsidy. One isolated instance of sponsorship was the 15 million crowns (£300,000) being given by Motorcorp to the Prague Spring Festival.

Again, four working groups discussed these matters under the leadership of Nicos Manolopoulos, the general manager of the new Athens Concert Hall in Greece, Sven-Gunnar Tillius from the Goteborgs Musiktheater, Neil Wallace (Deputy Director of Festivals in Glasgow) and Jeff Pivac (Director of Gallus International in Ljubljana).

The final day began with constructive working groups on Lobbying (led by Simon Mundy, Director of the National Campaign for the Arts in London), Negotation (led by Richard Pulford), Sponsorship (led by Martijn Sanders, managing director of the Concertgebouw of Amsterdam) and Marketing (led by Dagmar Hahn and Helmut Pauli).

Probably the most heart-stopping speech came from Ion Caramitru on 'Where will the changes in Europe lead?' Caramitru is Director of the Balandra Theatre in Bucharest and was introduced by Martine Baudin from Brussels as 'a man of freedom'. He is a charismatic actor and director who agreed with Sir Ian McKellen that he would better serve the cause of Arts Administrators in Europe to be present at the ISPAA conference than to be in Bucharest to welcome the National Theatre from Great Britain presenting *King Lear* and *Richard III*. Caramitru emphasised the difficulties of the new Parliament in Rumania attempting to sort out its problems just at the moment of the outset of the Gulf War. The realities of the present economic situation in central Europe meant that there were harsh realities to be faced by all arts organisations.

Creative artists, he pointed out, were always in the forefront of those seeking true freedom of individual expression. Any change to a system which had ruled for 45 years was obviously going to be very slow and, as a Romantic, he had rejected all approaches for him to become involved in any political party since he wished to remain with the theatre.

He was obviously concerned about the poverty of his nation, in that there was no money for the arts now that it had gained a freedom to interchange plays with the West and he pleaded that dramatists should accept currency in the country where works are performed.

The final lunch was held in the splendour of the Dobris Palace, built in 1745 some 35 kilometres outside Prague and set in unforgettable snow-bound scenery. Professor August Everding from Munich gave the last address in German on 'A Europe Without Cultural Frontiers', efficiently translated by Eckhard Heintz.

Richard Pulford referred to the constant emphasis on the strength of ISPAA members being a source of support and advice to each other. The enormous asset of personal contacts and improved communication between members was proving most constructive. An example given during the discussion was of Theatre Projects Consultants arranging for the new Administrator, the House Manager and all the new box office staff at the newly built Athens Concert Hall opening this year, to receive training under experienced staff in similar organisations in Great Britain.

Outside the formal sessions were a great number of special events including access to many of Prague's splendid theatres and its castle. Performances were available by the original Prague Mozart Company, the Gagman Group, the Russian Derevo Dance Group, the Dutch Dog Troep Theatre, the Chamber Orchestra of Joseph Suk, the Theatre on a Spring performing Shakespeare and the opera and ballet productions of the National Theatre.

One of the increasing problems with tourists in respect of the arts and entertainment is how to educate them without making theatre and concert-going appear at all pretentious or elitist. Allowing applause between movements might be quite acceptable but is a million light-years from the battery of flashlights experienced at *The Sleeping Beauty* in Prague's beautiful Smetana Theatre. A violinist like Nigel Kennedy's informal dress and even the London Symphony Orchestra's more relaxed dress for Summer Pops can be welcomed but not an audience entering and leaving during the BBC Scottish Symphony Orchestra playing a Haydn symphony in Athens, not to mention the attendants there eating sandwiches while standing at the exit doors during the concert.

A system of filling available seats immediately before a performance begins might be workable but not on the random system which seemed to be employed by attendants at the Magic Lantern Company of seating an audience quickly at random ignoring the actual seats booked.

Arts Administrators need to maintain and enforce very high standards of etiquette at concerts and audiences need to be trained to these standards for two main reasons – firstly as respect to the performers and secondly in basic onsideration for the remainder of the audience.

The next ISPAA Conference will be held in June in Los Angeles and the next European Conference will be held in January 1992 in Budapest. It will be interesting and important then to note what movement has taken place in the intervening 12 months in the proportions of income received by arts organisations from central and local government, the box office, sponsorship and all exploitation of product (by way of records, video, transfers of productions, posters, restaurant and bar facilities, and the numerous ways of earning income).

Finally, my personal plea is to ask all arts administrators to maximise income from ticket sales. The Gag Company in Prague plays to local audiences for very low admission prices on certain nights and on other nights play to tourists at higher prices. It was distressing to find that tickets for leading ballet and opera productions were fixed at such low top prices as 50 Crowns (about £1) which is all the local population can afford, but were available from ticket agencies to tourists at 300 Crowns (£6). No tourist would object to a top price for grand opera and ballet productions if that money was going to the performing company and Central European countries need to avoid finding that parasites of the arts are creaming off the healthy income which should be available to creative artists. The degenerative system of ticket touts in many western countries is not an example to be followed.

Getting In On The Act

The Stage, 4 December 2003

Hard on the heels of Robert Cogo-Fawcett's erudite account of the relationship between subsidised and commercial theatre comes the publication of the Theatres Trust *Act Now!* Report on modernising London's West End theatres.

Its cogent arguments for preserving the 40 commercial theatres in the West End, which produce some £200 million of tax revenues for the Treasury each year as well as generating more than £400 million on other aspects of the UK economy, support the fact that this is a key part of our national heritage as well as our largest invisible export. Visitors to the UK do not come here for the weather and, indeed, many countries with warm climates, seas and beaches are now frantically attempting to develop their cultural resources so that tourists have something to attract them in the evenings and out of season months.

The Theatres Trust has estimated a need of some £250 million to be spent over a 15-year period and this has obviously terrified some government ministers. The fact that the Lottery was inaugurated on the basis of all ministers and political parties swearing it would be used solely for cultural purposes has already been long-forgotten by party politicians.

Act Now! refers to "concern about the risk of Lottery or taxpayers' money going into private pockets" and this has been exercising the minds of accountants for many years in the various, aspects of show business. Until *Salad Days* was transferred half a century ago from the subsidised Bristol Old Vic – registered as a non-profit-distributing charity – to the Vaudeville Theatre by a commercial producer, the two worlds had remained separate. Since then the subsidised and commercial theatres have increasingly moved closer together. Cameron Mackintosh's funds made it possible to turn what would have been a standard regional theatre production of *My Fair Lady* at Leicester Haymarket in 1978 into a star-studded spectacle. This later toured the large regional touring theatres – with Arts Council of Great Britain guarantees against loss – and came into the Adelphi Theatre for a further year in 1979. This not only helped keep the large regional venues open for the Arts Council tours of its national opera and dance companies but generated profits for the theatre in Leicester, the Arts Council itself, and for Mackintosh. This pattern was repeated with the production of *Oklahoma!* at Leicester, on tour and subsequently at the Palace Theatre.

The meeting of the commercial and subsidised worlds has been furthered with the creation of the Theatre Investment Fund and the TKTS booking centre in Leicester Square, both with Arts Council England funds knowingly assisting commercial productions.

The Theatres Trust report suggests a number of ways which might be explored to tackle this problem. As long ago as 1955, I administered a financial solution for the old Comedy Theatre by which the commercial company which had purchased this then dilapidated venue financed the renovation by building an office block over the backstage dressing room accommodation and, furthermore, subsequent rents financially supported the running costs of the theatre. This scheme was later copied, mainly in American cities with their theatres exploiting air space.

Let's face the fact that it is unlikely that Arts Council of England (ACE) or the Lottery will change its attitude to the plight of commercial theatre buildings. However, the government at present appears to be willing to consider investment opportunities and a new body could well be set up to lend capital funds to assist in the essential work required to maintain the West End theatre infrastructure.

Mackintosh has thrown down the gauntlet in his announcement that he is to spend more than £30 million on his theatre buildings, already commencing with the Prince of Wales and Strand theatres. If these were regional, subsidised theatres, this benevolence would have been more than matched by Lottery funds. The unusual profits generated by successful long-running musicals cannot be generated by productions of plays and many stand-alone theatres such as the Playhouse, the Criterion, the Shaftesbury, the Haymarket or the Arts could never hope to produce such profits. The four 'drama houses' on Shaftesbury Avenue – the Lyric, the Apollo, Queens and Gielgud – have generated a total profit since 1945 which is less than the Lottery paid for the Royal Court.

However, a trust on the lines of the Theatre Investment Fund could be set up to lend the required funds for theatre renovations to be achieved over the 15 year period promulgated in the *Act Now!* Report.

My proposals (in a recent letter to *The Times*) were for commercial companies to build into all their annual trading accounts a properly calculated depreciation reserve and this could enable the funds to be repaid to the Investment Fund to ensure its future. At long last, Westminster and other London councils are starting to address the problems of cleaning up our environment and the police and other authorities are matching these efforts. It makes sense for the circle to be completed.

The *Act Now!* Report certainly reminds us what a wonderful heritage we have in our West End theatres. They are miracles of compression, bringing audiences and actors together to experience great drama and music. I commend the report's summary and conclusions and its final page 'Protecting the Future' is essential reading. This problem will not go away and if the government ignores the situation, it will get progressively worse and the country will lose its golden nest egg.

Regions At Risk

The Stage, 31 July 2003

My recent features on the problems of West End theatres being dominated by financiers and business people rather than actors, producers and directors, leads one to wonder whether regional theatres are able to resist this downward spiral. In the past, drama in the regions was divided between what was available in the large commercial Stoll-Moss/Howard & Wyndham circuits and the 40 or 50 subsidised repertory companies in Britain – such as in Lancaster and Crewe, Northampton and Worcester, York and Worthing as well as 12 in Scotland and 6 in Wales.

Once the Arts Council of Great Britain decided to terminate most of the regional repertory work, drama became a rare commodity for regional audiences. Vast lottery funds were made available to renovate or rebuild many of the theatres sorely in need of restoration. But those in charge of lottery money did not appear to be in contact with those responsible for subsidising the performing companies occupying these venues, many of which were allowed to slide into liquidation.

When Peter Longman, now director of the Theatres Trust, was administering the Arts Council's Housing the Arts funds, one of the important criteria was that those theatres in receipt of capital funds should also be in receipt of adequate revenue funds. This was so that proper annual provision could be made in subsequent years to replace the equipment, furnishings and renovations without having to resort to yet further applications.

Unfortunately, all too rarely were proper assessments made of the cost of running the new or refurbished buildings so that, lo and behold, the window-cleaning bill for the façade of the new Birmingham Repertory Theatre was found to be more than the entire cost of running the old Rep under Barry Jackson.

I always hoped that these lessons would be learned but, wait for it, the superb work of Philip Hedley at the Theatre Royal, Stratford East is now in jeopardy because no one seems to have anticipated that the cost of running the refurbished theatre is so high.

I can only hope that the companies now running the few regional theatres we have left, whether commercial or subsidised, are setting aside proper reserves for repairs and renewals. I am tired of pointing out what accountants are always having to emphasise – that the cost of the annual depreciation of such items as seating and carpets are as much part of the annual expenditure as the lighting and heating.

So, where are the regional theatres going? The most exciting work is still being done where playwrights such as Alan Ayckbourn at Scarborough or directors like Braham Murray at Manchester's Royal Exchange are in charge. Certainly not in the large theatres taking in touring product in the hope that vast profits can accrue from popcorn and bar receipts.

Following the example set all those years ago by Laurence Olivier at Chichester, Peter Hall is now launching a 12-week summer season at the Theatre Royal, Bath, to include a newly discovered play by D H Lawrence, Noel Coward's *Design for Living*, Harold Pinter's *Betrayal*, a transfer of *Cuckoos* from the Barbican Pit and *As You Like It*, which it is hoped will transfer to the newly-refurbished Hackney Empire in October. Hall then plans next year to run a permanent company at Kingston Theatre.

At present there are larger audiences attending tours to the regional receiving houses. It seems surprising that shows can take more money in a week at Southampton or the Lowry Centre in Salford than in a West End theatre.

No wonder that David Pugh was able to shout from the rooftops that the three actors in *Art* could bring in almost a quarter of a million pounds to the Mayflower box office in a week in Southampton.

All this leaves the regional theatres in much the same state as we find the West End. There are the big musicals and revivals but hardly any new British drama. The days when commercial producers found new plays in the regional repertory houses have gone, as have the days when there was an abundance of new plays finding their way into repertory seasons once they had finished their London runs. The 'grey suits' have sapped the life out of British theatre.

A Helping Hand

The Stage, 9 October 2003

The Regional Theatre Initiative is spending £400,000 on helping to develop a career path for directors and other innovative talent in regional theatres throughout England and Scotland. The Esmee Fairbairn Foundation is making grants of £26 million for arts and heritage, education, environment and social development projects across the UK.

The programme is based on the judgement of artistic directors at theatres who wish to mount plays with young directors given the chance to mount a major production. So far theatres working in the scheme include Birmingham Rep, Salisbury Playhouse, West Yorkshire Playhouse, Manchester Royal Exchange, Sheffield Crucible and Nottingham Playhouse.

Unfortunately for recent correspondents to *The Stage* – Anthony Melnikoff on September 11th – there are few new plays included in the recent decisions. The productions chosen are *As You Like It*, *Much Ado About Nothing*, *Twelfth Night*, Arthur Miller's *A View From the Bridge*, Euripides' *Iphigenia*, Max Frisch's *Andorra*, David Rudkin's *Afore Night Comes* and Edward Bond's *The Sea*.

Perhaps this is because new playwrights have been conditioned to writing scripts with two characters and one set, having been told that new plays are too financially risky if submitted with a cast of 12 and three sets. The Regional Theatres Initiative is designed to foster young directors working with a team of designers, stage managers and house management and with a cast larger than they would normally afford.

The Arts Council of Great Britain used to run a scheme of giving regional theatres guarantees against loss on the first production of a new play or even for the second production of a new play.

I continue to hope that someone will revive the idea of dedicating a London season to regional theatre work. I have written before in *The Stage* about the season of productions given at St James's Theatre in 1948 from Sheffield, Liverpool, Bristol and Birmingham Repertory Companies. There was also a guest repertory season ten years later with four new plays hosted at the Royal Court Theatre in July 1958. Glasgow Citizens' Theatre presented *Gay Landscape* by George Munro, of which *The Stage* critic wrote: "The performances were impressive, particularly by Annette Crosbie and Fulton Mackay, showing London is not the only place where good acting and teamwork are to be found."

The Belgrade Theatre in Coventry presented the first production of Arnold Wesker's *Chicken Soup with Barley* with Frank Finlay, Alfred Lynch, Patsy Byrne, Anthony Valentine, Richard Briers and Charmian Eyre.

The season also included new productions of *Dear Augustine* by Alison MacLeod from Leatherhead Thorndike Theatre and *The Private Prosecutor* by Thomas Wiseman from Salisbury Arts Theatre.

It is a pity that we have to wait almost half a century for a similar season to be presented in London.

The financial pages of newspapers have been filled recently with reports of the future of Time Warner and EMI. The issues involving international copyright tend to bring a glazed look to the eyes of performing artists, although the theft of intellectual property concerns all creative people in show business. And it is just that – theft.

In the entertainment industry, the protection of intellectual property rights is the lifeblood of all who work in the creation of a production. In a world of constantly changing technology and boundless opportunities, the price is constant vigilance and continual adaptation as new challenges arise.

One is reminded of the plans of the Marx Brothers to follow up the success of *A Night At The Opera* with *A Night in Casablanca*, which was to be a spoof of the Warner Brothers' 1942 classic *Casablanca*, but broadening its focus to become a parody of wartime melodramas. Warner Brothers' legal representatives objected to their proposed use of the word *Casablanca*, which they maintained demeaned their film. Groucho replied by objecting to Warner Brothers using the word 'Brothers', which the Marx family had used for many years before Warner Brothers came into existence.

Luckily, titles cannot be patented and indeed, with the increased use of the internet, even ideas cannot be controlled. Thus it is becoming all but impossible for creative people – writers, composers, dramatists, choreographers – to protect their original work.

Downloading for free is no longer regarded to be the fraud which it really is. Luckily, in spite of the photocopier, no one appears to be downloading books in huge quantities. It is obviously cheaper to buy a paperback of *War and Peace* rather than attempt to download it.

However, many copyright issues remain to be resolved. James Bell, one of Australia's leading commercial and entertainment lawyers, addressed the ISPA Congress in Birmingham in 1995 on these issues and one gained the impression that a number of delegates came away feeling that lawyers were being a bit alarmist about these problems. Eight years later, we are all beginning to realise how wrong we were. We did not anticipate the ingenuity of those who would seek to profit from the theft of copyright music and its dissemination over the internet.

Lawyers are often maligned without justification. In the entertainment industry they are all too often regarded as an impediment. What appear to be simple exchanges of letters become costly contractual negotiations. The UK investment contract for the original production of *Art* ran to some four pages. Its transfer to New York required an investment contract of some 81 after the US lawyers became involved.

However, if deals are not set up correctly and are not properly documented at the outset they can fall apart and may eventually lead to costly disputes.

Some years ago at Malta, I found large posters advertising a school performance of *Miss Saigon*, together with the London logo. I expected Cameron Mackintosh to turn his lawyers on them. Certainly, the headmaster and the school governors should have known about copyright and royalties.

However, it transpired that Mackintosh's dear mother had told her Maltese relatives: "Of course, Cameron won't mind." However, they have not done it again.

All arts management training courses should contain the relevant aspect of law as an essential element, since all artists require an overview of the legal framework in which they will work. They need to know the protection that is available to them for the intellectual property they create and the obligations that bind them. The syllabus should cover such subjects as defamation, piracy of recordings, contractual arrangements, copyright and trade marking.

This is no different from the sensible requirement for all artists to be taught the rudiments of finance, so that they know how to deal with their earnings, income tax problems, cash flow requirements and other core principles. The days when new, young artists were ripped off by unscrupulous parasites in this profession should have long gone. This was one of the reasons Paul McCartney devoted much effort and cash towards the establishment of the Liverpool Institute for the Performing Arts.

In the world of pop music, it appears to be too late to prevent the widespread downloading of songs and to invoke any laws in respect of intellectual property.

Perhaps we simply have to move on. The old 78s became albums and cassette-tapes became CDs. But perhaps all recorded music has become a thing of the past. This might bode well for live performance. Thomas Beecham believed the wireless would leave the concert halls deserted, but perhaps they are going to come back into popularity and the lure of live performances will reign supreme as in the days of Mozart. Thus, composers and musicians and singers will need to produce new songs every day or every week rather than an album every year. This will herald a new and exciting era for the whole of the music industry.

However, in the world of international copyright, many issues remain unresolved. We must all, therefore, support the enforcement of intellectual property rights and the improvement of its recognition worldwide, for the benefit of all those creative artists in the entertainment industry and the preservation of their livelihoods.

Precious Preservation

The Stage, 6 May 2004.

Unlike so many other aspects of life the theatre is ephemeral. Films are usually always available and with tapes, discs and other modern technical devices so are television and radio programmes. However, a newly released DVD of the New York production of *Fosse* has opened my eyes to a growing market for such theatrical productions being made available in this way. It has been the case for many years that certain London productions could be recorded purely for archive records. Usually this has meant that, with special permission, a camera could be installed at the back of the auditorium to record a performance.

However, in New York, specific arrangements are negotiated whereby a special performance is given in front of an audience, with a number of cameras and specialised sound and lighting, so that a balanced film of a production can be professionally produced. Obviously, the editing will often dictate which part of the action the viewer is concentrated on rather than simply giving an overall view of the entire stage. This can be beneficial in highlighting certain intimate moments although it may rob a theatregoer of deciding what part of the action he or she might choose to watch.

Edward Albee recently commented on the DVD release of his play *A Delicate Balance* by explaining that the corruption of the film industry should not be allowed to impose on a serious work. I see no reason for a play to be altered, adapted, cut or reshaped. However, Edward Albee welcomed such filmed versions and would like to see all of his 27 plays recorded if he could have some control over the editing, direction and production.

The release of Albee's *A Delicate Balance* is, in fact, a 1975 filmed version of the 1966 Pulitzer Prize-winning play directed by Tony Richardson and starring Katherine Hepburn and Paul Scofield. Similar releases include Chekhov's *The Three Sisters* directed by Laurence Olivier, Eugene O'Neill's *The Iceman Cometh* with Lee Marvin and Arthur Miller's *Death Of A Salesman* with Dustin Hoffman and John Malkovich. The 1966 production of *Death Of A Salesman* is also available on DVD with Lee J. Cobb reprising his original Broadway performance.

No doubt all these DVDs are of particular interest to theatregoers rather than viewers used to television and cinemas where one is conditioned to expect short scenes with great emphasis on the picture rather than the text and/or music. There are also a number of plays by Shakespeare, originally shown on

BBC television, now available on DVD including *Othello* with Anthony Hopkins and Bob Hoskins, *The Taming Of The Shrew* with John Cleese and *A Midsummer Night's Dream* with Helen Mirren.

A unique project has been the filming of 19 of Samuel Beckett's plays including *Catastrophe*, directed by David Mamet, with a mute John Gielgud on the stage at 96, no doubt his last performance, alongside Harold Pinter.

Strangely, what is ephemeral about show business is the life of production companies. In commerce and industry, Unilever and Shell can go on forever as international conglomerates. Film Companies like Universal, Twentieth Century Fox and MGM can survive as such, even if now owned by banks. But theatre producers are usually only as good as their last production and last as long as they are in charge. There is no Charles B. Cochran Ltd. or Henry Sherek Company now in being. H.M. Tennent did not live much longer than Binkie Beaumont and where is Howard & Wyndham and Stoll-Moss as far as production is concerned?

Architectural partnerships might well continue after their founder retires and law firms continue when their original creators die. But it is fascinating to debate what happens when, we hope not, David Pugh or Michael Codron fall into the Thames or Cameron Mackintosh into a Scottish loch. Certainly their existing productions can continue to be exploited but who can take over their creativity? And if there is anyone around who could do so, would they not wish to do so through their own Company and not through a David Pugh Ltd. or Cameron Mackintosh Productions?

Further, this leads one to debate what these production companies are worth if to be available for sale on the open market.

This is similar to the debate as to how much one should insure theatre buildings for. The Royal National Theatre is no doubt covered by a Government indemnity; but, if not, how much would one insure it for in the case of its burning down? Or if it were to be sold who on earth would purchase it without the enormous Arts Council annual subsidy? What, in fact, is its market value? Answers on a postcard please, to the Editor of *The Stage*.

In the meantime, the Coliseum has been restored to its Frank Matcham glory so that the English National Opera can prove that it is one of the world's leading opera companies. Does this get headlines in the popular dailies? Further Lottery money went to the Lowry Centre in Salford which has played to packed houses for drama, comedy, thrillers and dance companies since it opened. Do the red-top papers mention it? Government grants to the BBC enable it to produce such films as *Billy Elliot* which smashed box office records and won international awards. Do the tabloids praise the BBC? Three questions with one answer to each of them – Never!

But one film, *Sex Lives Of The Potato Men* savaged by film critics, probably correctly and rightly, and it reaches headlines in the tabloids - not a mention on page 3 or 5 or 7 or the film page, but headlines, designed to whip public reaction into a frenzy against any subsidies to the entertainment world, our largest invisible export.

This demonstrates partly a desire to sell newspapers by giving their readers what they want, but also a fundamental ignorance of how the entertainment business operates. Even we in show business are continuously surprised at possible flops which turn into smash-hits and vice-versa. Do we go by our first instincts or are we persuaded by colleagues against our better judgement? If we knew the answers to all these questions we would all be millionaires. Sir Cameron Mackintosh tells us that he only puts on shows he would want to see. If the public flocks to *Cats*, *Phantom* and *Les Mis* all is well. If they ignore *Café Puccini*, *Moby Dick* and *Martin Guerre* – well, that's show business.

Sometimes I have rejected a proposed production on first reading the script. Then I am told it will star Vanessa Redgrave so would I change my mind? And then I am asked if it were to be directed by Stephen Daldry would I change my mind? Further, it is decided to open it in seven weeks at Wyndham's Theatre will I then go for it? So I weaken and admit I may have been wrong. It opens to the critics damning it, audiences staying away and the show closes: And I think "But that's what I first thought when I rejected it!"

I noted that the barrage of criticism of *Sex Lives Of The Potato Men* has prompted the call for Lottery money to be routed away from film-makers to distributors. There is no doubt that something should be done about our distribution system which side-lines such brilliant films as *The Mother* making it impossible for filmgoers to see Anne Reid's superb performance. We shall, however, see her this year at Chichester in *Out Of This World.*

However, this reminds me of what happened when Lord Goodman arrived as Chairman of the Arts Council of Great Britain astounded that no funds were being channelled to Literature. In no time at all a Literature Director was appointed and a Literature Advisory Panel was set up. At its first meeting it resolved to spend its funds on bursaries to writers to give them time to write. At the end of the first year the Panel members reviewed all the works that had been produced but were aghast that none had been published. So the second year's allocation of funds was channelled to publishers to help get all this new work published. At the end of the second year the Panel was faced with all these published works not being found on booksellers' shelves. So the third year found the Literature Panel channelling money to assist new bookshops opening in towns without any or supporting the stocking of new books in shops otherwise ignoring them. Finally, in the fourth year the Panel returned to giving bursaries to writers to buy time to write.

Now we find the Inland Revenue has decided without any warning to change the rules about investment in film-making. Did the tabloids run any headlines on the new Jude Law film *Tulip Fever* collapsing with vast numbers of people being laid off. Or was the collapse of the John Malkovich film *The Libertine* mentioned on page 15 of the red-tops with last year's £600 million worth of British films simply stopping overnight? Some 40 British films will now collapse - films like *Notting Hill*, *Four Weddings And A Funeral* and *Calendar Girls*. But all this is simply forgotten in the media rush to headline one dire, despicable failure.

On the Wrong Track

The Stage, 29 April 2004

I must again be in a minority of one to hear with a sinking heart that Birmingham Rep. are housing a satirical musical about the war on terrorism and also that the Royal National Theatre has commissioned David Hare to write a documentary, *Stuff Happens* about the lead-up to the war in Iraq. I have only just recovered from the evenings spent in the Tricycle documenting the Hutton Report, *Justifying War* and in the Cottesloe watching actors declaiming what I had already read in so many newspapers about the four train crash disasters in recent years.

I am full of genuine sympathy with people caught up in all these calamities and it is only right that the present theatre should reflect the current political scene.

Alistair Beaton wrote a most amusing play about the present political climate and *Feelgood* transferred from Hampstead to the Garrick Theatre. His new satirical musical will feature Bush and Blair as a singing duo celebrating their decisions from September 11th to the reconstruction of Iraq. *Follow My Leader* is at Birmingham Repertory Theatre and transfers to Hampstead on 23rd April.

What concerns me about all these staged documentaries is whether they are good drama. I suppose they are good for the theatre if they ring the box office tills. But they appear to preach to the converted and do not reach the unconverted. The audiences at the Cottesloe for *The Permanent Way* all applaud what they have already read in the Guardian or Independent about the Southall, Hatfield and Potters Bar carnages. But I did not note any Sun or Mirror readers in that audience.

What I believe the theatre needs is well-constructed plays derived from important social matters. If Shaw had written a dialogue between surgeons, doctors and dentists outlining the problems of the medical profession, we should not now be presenting it, whereas we still admire in *The Doctor's Dilemma* or *You Never Can Tell*. A diatribe about VD from Ibsen would have robbed us of *Ghosts*. The problems the public has in dealing with the legal profession were superbly dramatised by Terence Rattigan in *The Winslow Boy* and again in *Cause Célèbre*.

Journey's End has been so successful currently at the Comedy that it is transferring to the Playhouse on 3rd May. This superbly crafted indictment of war was written by R.C. Sherriff in 1929 and had it been written as a quick fix documentary in 1918 we would have been robbed of a classic piece of theatre.

All these plays required hard work in their construction and real investment in time in their dramatisation. In the end, these plays reached vast radio and television audiences and see constant revivals in the cinema after being turned into film classics. Thus they reach the audiences that the Cottesloe and Hampstead do not reach. If one is simply looking for something to fill those stages and their seats then all well and good. But if there really is a genuine political agenda behind them they have to be presented more palatably to the general public.

David Edgar's fascinating two plays comprising *Continental Divide* ingeniously combine a political drama within a family concept. Both *Mothers Against* and *Daughters Of The Revolution* achieve what is most difficult in such endeavours. The playwright has to spend a great deal of thought in containing a political theme within a well constructed play but without losing the essential political drive. Rattigan achieved it in *The Winslow Boy* as did Priestley with *An Inspector Calls*. It is gratifying to note that these plays are regularly chosen as set-books in schools and universities. I doubt if *The Permanent Way* or *Stuff Happens* will ever achieve that status simply because they are quick, topical pieces of journalism. I write this with great sadness because with more time and the creativity which David Hare has regularly proved he has, such plays could be as important as his superb trilogy *Racing Demon*, *Murmuring Judges* and *The Absence Of War* which served to analyse the church, the law and the Labour Party, rather than our Railway Network.

But I must be wrong about what current theatregoers demand. After the Birmingham opening the critics forecast that "the Barbican should be packed", but it wasn't – and *The Permanent Way* was – so perhaps we are just more interested in our railways than the American constitution.

7 MUSICALS

Are Musicals More Fun?

Tony's piece points out the different approaches that public and performers have to the musical: some people are huge fans of the genre, and Dress Circle, London's best-known showbiz shop, is devoted to recordings (and videos and books) from musicals. Similarly, some performers love to be in song and dance pieces, others (as is the case with Jonathan Pryce in the 1990 Stage article) just see them as another job rather than a favoured art form.

It is certainly the case that there's something of a knee-jerk reaction against musicals: how often have you heard or read that 'there are too many musicals in London'? Yet what theatregoer would ever say 'there are too many theatres in London?' Better a theatre with a musical than a dark theatre, and in any case, most of the theatres where musicals are staged – the Dominion and Drury Lane, for example – are now seen as too large for anything other than a full-scale musical to be staged there, so it isn't a case of musicals 'stealing' a theatre from a potential play.

2004 is going to be a very musical year for London – with Andrew Lloyd Webber's latest, *The Woman in White*, opening in the later part of the year, along with the stage version of *Mary Poppins* and *The Producers*. There is also a stage musical of *The Lord of the Rings* scheduled for 2005, so the musical, as an art form, is still very much alive and kicking.

Musicals are notoriously expensive to stage, costing several times the price of a straight show, largely because they usually involve a larger cast and more set changes, but also because of the need for a band. This cost is itself something of a quality control device, as a producer has to be fairly confident that a show will do well. There are still some notable disasters of course – like the aptly-named *Money to Burn* at The Venue in 2003, which closed after only a few days.

Can musicals reach the heights of emotion that straight plays do? This question, touched on in the article, is still hotly debated. Music is highly atmospheric, and supporters of classical music and opera will claim that a few bars of music can reach the human heart far more quickly and effectively than the equivalent number of words, and there's something in that, but then poetry is also a highly effective shorthand way of reaching the emotions, and lines of

Shakespeare are as moving as a burst of Puccini.

Whether Rodgers and Hammerstein, Noel Coward or Stephen Sondheim can create the same emotional impact as Puccini remains debatable, and this is likely always to be the case. What is sure, however, is that a good musical can pack in the coach-loads in the way that very few plays possibly could, and the feel-good factor from Trevor Nunn's production of Cole Porter's *Anything Goes*, first at the National, then at Drury Lane, beats most 'straight' productions hands down, however funny they may have been.

A more effective debate, and which rarely surfaces, would be about the *type* of musical on offer: why can't there be revivals of British musicals rather than endless revivals of American ones? Why can't we see any one of the string of hits that Ivor Novello wrote (*Glamorous Night*, *Careless Rapture*, *The Dancing Years*, *King's Rhapsody*, and more) back on a London stage. Or Coward's *Bitter Sweet*?

American musicals are wonderful, and both revivals (*Anything Goes*) and new shows (*The Producers*) are very welcome, but many British musicals deserve to be revived, too. The theatre that has the best track record in staging new British musicals is the National, which premiered Styles and Drewe's *Honk!* and gave a major platform to the extant production of *Jerry Springer – the Opera*. Hopefully Nicholas Hytner will continue this tradition and help promote some more new British musicals over the course of his time as Artistic Director.

When it comes to performers' attitude to musicals, their approach will inevitably be affected by their ability to sing, and in the course of a long career a performer known mainly for straight plays might become better-known for musicals or *vice versa*. Michael Crawford was always an excellent comedy performer, including in the stage musical *Billy* at Drury Lane in the early 1970s, but it wasn't until *The Phantom of the Opera* at Her Majesty's in 1986 that became internationally famous as a romantic lead in a musical. Similarly, not many of the public who flocked to see Dame Judi Dench in David Hare's *Amy's View*, or *The Breath of Life*, are aware that as a young woman she starred as Sally Bowles in a stage production of *Cabaret* produced by Theatre Projects at the Palace Theatre in 1968.

Musicals will always be a part of the London scene, they are rightly a popular art form and, largely thanks to Cameron Mackintosh, as both a producer and the sponsor of a professorship at Oxford, they are increasingly taken seriously as an art form. Intellectual snobbery and sheer tradition will mean some people will always see performing in a musical as somehow less worthwhile or serious than appearing in a straight play, but such a distinction is in effect unworkable and should be seen as personal opinion rather than objective fact.

PW

Is it a sign of current show business trends that the Oxford University lectures on musicals attracted standing room only for directors and producers but did not fill all the seats for the performers?

Certainly the second session of the Trinity Term at St Catherine's College deserved a full house, even at the start of a holiday weekend, when Mark Steyn superbly chaired Jonathan Pryce, Julia McKenzie, Philip Quast and Patti LuPone discussing their influence on the writing and construction of musicals in which they had appeared.

For nearly two hours these four personalities poured forth their eloquent observations on musicals with which they have been associated – as diverse as *Anything Goes, Evita, Miss Saigon, Les Misérables, Sunday In The Park With George, Follies, Into The Woods* and *Side By Side With Sondheim.*

Interestingly, all had also appeared in straight dramas and comedies and all agreed that it was easier to keep their performances fresh and sustain their characterisations in long-run musicals than in the straight theatre.

"Even after a year, when that orchestra starts, it elevates you into a wonderful performance – a release of emotions" – and Jonathan Pryce confessed that, whereas in Shakespeare and Chekhov he found himself counting the performances ("half performances in the interval!"). Even after six months in *Miss Saigon* he was finding new and exciting things in the song and dance and characterisation.

Indeed, he had asked a psychiatrist why he was *not* going mad and apparently research is now being undertaken into the discovery that there is a confirmed area of the brain which is used only for singing. Pryce even reported that during their studies into conditions in Vietnam it was indicated that in their worst plight the population often communicated only in song.

Although LuPone nearly fell off her seat laughing at this, it did remind one of *Ghetto* and the fact that much great music has emanated from tragedy.

Mark Steyn opened the questioning with the comment that before there were writers, composers and directors, there were performers. First and foremost there were personalities – the Ethel Mermans, Mary Martins, Gwen Verdons, Gertrude Lawrences, Chita Riveras, Liza Minellis, Barbra Streisands – (Julia McKenzie would not be drawn on the attractions of the great female parts in musicals not necessarily being available in the straight theatre!)

In those days composers wrote musicals for the stars, knew their vocal range and acting capabilities; the conductors understood the individual artists' needs so that without mikes the artists would not be drowned by the orchestra. The stars then projected the show into the audience, whereas Philip Quast explained that with *Sunday In The Park With George* you have to let the audience *into* the musical.

The question of the size and nature of the theatres next came under review and Quast emphasised that audiences' expectations can be different between those seeing *Les Misérables* in a clinical modern auditorium in Australia and those walking into the wonderful old ambience of the Palace in London. However, he liked large spaces although they can be difficult to conquer.

McKenzie cited the very difficult concrete areas of the Olivier for *Guys and Dolls* but once she had embraced the space in her arms it was superb for an epic musical. It was emphasised that producers must recognise the needs of artists and it was unfortunate that on tour one needed the Monday night (just when the critics were in!) to size up the venue and the audience.

McKenzie confessed that her favourite musical house was Her Majesty's (where she appeared in *On The Twentieth Century*) and her favourite comedy house was the Globe (now called the Gielgud) Theatre. LuPone explained that actors can get very angry with producers when not enough thought is put into the transfer of a successful show from a suitable fringe or off-Broadway house into an unsuitable one in the West End or on Broadway. "Hits are more fragile than flops!" seemed a significant comment to be ringing in our ears in respect of long runs as well as of transfers.

There was a question about whether characterisation demanded as much attention from artists in musicals and Pryce explained that sung-through musicals are no different from Shakespeare, where the metre carried you through so long as you maintain the truth of your performance. However, he considered that much research was needed into the stress level for actors – which was very different when you were nightly committing murder as Macbeth and your wife was dying at each performance – whereas a musical tends to release your emotions.

McKenzie considered that musicals were very different from each other – her characterisation when appearing with Bob Hoskins in *Guys and Dolls* needed re-appraising when he left the cast; but with some musicals "If you think, you die!" Pryce admitted that he daren't think about his dancing and

LuPone referred to the singer who was worried about her characterisation only to be told by Jule Styne "Just sing the goddam song for chrissake!"

A great divergence of opinion emerged in relation to matinee audiences. Pryce considered they were real people who wanted to be there whereas LuPone considered them to the blue-rinse 'bridge and tunnel' crowd who couldn't hear and were largely asleep. Perhaps this reflected the difference between British and American matinee audiences.

It was some way into the afternoon before the question of the artist's influence on the writing and construction of musicals brought the discussion back to the *raison d'être* of the session. Quast reported that Sondheim delivered the finished project and would not allow changes, even correcting an 'a' for 'the'. However, Sondheim knows exactly what he is producing and musically gives the artist thinking space.

LuPone reminded us that Ethel Merman often demanded changes to songs and Pryce admitted that he had written some (not many!) of the lyrics of *Miss Saigon*. One particular moment needed four extra lines for an artist's change and Pryce had suggested them.

Cameron Mackintosh reminded us that the most quoted lyrics from *Cats* were by Richard Stilgoe and not T S Eliot and that three important songs in *Les Misérables* ('Stars', 'Bring Him Home' and 'Dog Eats Dog') were written at the request of the actors in rehearsal who felt that the through-action was too shallow at those moments.

Inevitably with Steyn's presence, there was reference to whether musicals were now attracting more respect from the press. McKenzie reminded everyone that a comedy performer was considered to be even lower than a musical performer. Pryce considered that his performance in *Miss Saigon* was "just another job – last time I was with the RSC, this time I'm singing".

There was discussion about the recreation of original productions. LuPone agreed that although they all considered that the New York production of *Evita* was a faithful recreation of the original, it had obviously acquired the hard edge which American performers develop from the hard edge of living in New York. Further, once Hal Prince had recreated another *Evita* in Los Angeles he returned to the New York one and changed that in the light of the images created by the West Coast performers.

Quast admitted that he and Maria Friedman had agreed not to look at the video or listen to the cast album of *Sunday In The Park* while rehearsing the National Theatre production so they were not influenced by the performances of the original creators.

The afternoon ended with a few hopes for the future – LuPone looked forward to when someone would write for her *The Carmen Miranda Story* and McKenzie would love to find a really funny musical with comedy in the music – in fact, musical comedy!

Pryce had earlier in the afternoon been taught carefully by LuPone how to create a standing ovation and he managed to achieve it for all four performers and Mark Steyn.

Producing a Musical

The Stage, 3 May 1990

THE STAGE

Has the musical finally come of age now that it has reached the hallowed College of St Catherine at the University of Oxford? It took me almost a decade to pioneer the Department of Arts Policy and Management at the City University, now successfully running M.A., Ph.D., M.Phil., and diploma courses developed so superbly by Professor John Pick with over 120 students a year.

The Cameron Mackintosh Visiting Professor of Contemporary Theatre, Stephen Sondheim, has completed the Hilary term of the inaugural year with the fifth and final session. The last session was chaired by Melvyn Bragg with David Aukin, Cameron Mackintosh and Andre Ptasznski leading a lively discussion on Producing in Musical Theatre.

The earlier sessions had been on A History of the Musical Theatre, Lighting and Stage Design in Musical Theatre, and Orchestration, Musical Direction and Sound Design. This final session pleased the three producers in that it opened to a packed house and the questions and answers came thick and fast for two hours after which members of the audience queued to speak to the distinguished panel members, many wanting to thrust scripts, tapes and videos on them, even though Cameron Mackintosh pleaded that he had "retired"!

Indeed, it was perhaps disappointing that there were so many questions which proved to be variations on 'where can I get my show on?'. It seems amazing that so many writers and composers still think there is a mysterious key which will unlock the door to a four-year West End or Broadway success. Again and again, David Aukin (Executive Director of the National Theatre) stressed that a writer can only produce he/she really feels impelled to and that a producer can only respond to what appeals to him/her.

Cameron Mackintosh emphasised that he produced what he liked and Andre Ptasznski (Producer of *Return To The Forbidden Planet*) explained that he started as an ASM for a student production of *Loot* in the very Bernard Sunley Lecture Theatre in which we were sitting. There is no magic answer to so many of the questions.

On the provinces: The 'regions' have currently got more musicals than ever with *Evita*, *Cats*, *42nd Street*, *Chess*, *Joseph*, and *Show Boat* all on tour. A lady from East Anglia was told that it was bereft of major tours because of the financial policy of the theatre at Norwich.

On *Follies*: Cameron did not propose a Broadway production after the 'successful' West End production had lost 40% of its capital.

On 'hype': The producers asserted that this was done by the media. In fact, Cameron asserted that musicals like *Phantom* and *Miss Saigon* almost needed the hype damping down since they had taken off on their own. This was exacerbated by the touts who, whatever safeguards were attempted, had bought millions of pounds worth of tickets in advance of the opening of *Aspects of Love*.

On subsidised theatre: Generally, the producers considered that new large-scale musical were the province of the independent producers since the subsidised theatres had to provide a service to their regions offering a balanced programme which might include a revival of a musical just as one might revive a classic. David Aukin maintained that "putting on a new musical is like chasing the Holy Grail. I am amazed at the risks Cameron takes …"(Cameron: "So am I!").

On the complexity of musicals: Unlike a play, one has to deal with so many departments – the book, the lyrics, the music, the sound, the set, the costumes, the lighting, the direction, the choreography, the finance – and finding a theatre. Cameron maintained that once he was satisfied with the book, lyrics and music he expected to take at least three years to the first preview. It was admitted that there were no theatres left in London or New York available for new large-scale musicals.

On investors: The producers did not really know why these mad people poured their money into the theatre since seven out of every nine shows in the West End do not recoup their capital. Andre explained the problem of attempting to raise the capital at the right time – when the stars have been engaged but no theatre booked? One simply has to close one's eyes, gulp and launch into a production hoping that the capital will eventually be found. One investor had paid £25,000 in the hope he's to have tea with Pamela Stephenson …followed by a whip round of those who didn't want to take tea with…

On finance: It should have come as no surprise that the budgets for musicals had risen considerably in the past 20 years and that they also varied according to size – from £250,000 to £3million (*Miss Saigon*). There were specific questions as to which were the largest items in the budget for particular musicals and the responses varied from (i) publicity, the set and rehearsals (*The Forbidden Planet*), to (ii) artists, set and costumes (for *Sunday In The Park With George*) and (iii) the set (one-third of the cost), rehearsals and auditions (£250,000) for *Miss Saigon*.

On critics: In respect of musicals, do they operate for better or worse? David Aukin: "Well, certainly they do one or the other". Cameron thought they were brilliant and perceptive when they agreed with you and stupid and misled when they disagreed with you! Obviously no-one wanted to rise to this bait.

But again and again, questioners directly and indirectly returned to the problem of getting "my music, my songs, my play, my script" produced. One really constructive piece of advice came from Cameron. Don't spend money on expensive tapes with a full orchestra. Songs sung recognisably with a piano are sufficient; usually a complex orchestration merely disguises the inherent emptiness of the score.

No doubt it was difficult for many in the audience to be highly critical of the personal opinion of the man who has donated so much of his private fortune to such causes as this particular academic venture. So punches were apparently pulled by members of the audience such as veiled observations that *Shadowlands* was more moving than *Miss Saigon* or that certain plays appealed to the mind and heart more than certain musicals. There was further criticism that modern musicals did not really come to grips with current problems of civilisation. David Aukin cited *Ghetto* as being as relevant to human problems as *Bent*. Further, Cameron argued that nothing could be dealing more head-on with current human problems than *Miss Saigon*. However, one writer in the audience maintained that this was not dealing with the everyday problems of an individual in modern society (I was surprised that no-one here quoted *Company*) and Cameron pointed out that the music and choreography of *West Side Story* had not dated, whereas the book has dated as was likely with the book of any musical dealing with current social problems.

There were further implied assertions that what might have been originally a great ensemble musical like *Les Misérables* became less than 'great art' by having become *Les Misérables* PLC and it was pointed out in response that Ricordi had marketed Puccini's operas in a similar way with ice-cream boys on bicycles whistling the popular arias.

What is perhaps of concern is that the University academics have not yet indicated that they are prepared to enter into serious debate about musicals. Now that the university bastions have succumbed to taking Mackintosh's cash and creating A Visiting Professorship for Stephen Sondheim they owe it to us all to be ready to assess musicals using the same criteria as for other art forms. It is, after all, half a century since in the United States Pulitzer prizes recognised Rodgers and Hammerstein as well as Arthur Miller.

What we need to do is to assess why a certain formation of notes (B, G, B, G, A, F, G, D, G, D, F) which make up *Un bel di, vedremo levarsi un fil di fumo* is regarded as great art whereas a similar group of notes which form *The Last Night of the World* is "just a musical". Why is the libretto of *Madame Butterfly* ("One fine day we'll notice a thread of smoke arising") is part of operatic history to be studied at Oxford but the libretto of *Miss Saigon* ("A cry that tells us love goes on and on...") is simply a part of a West End 'show'?

If academics maintain one cannot dissect an opera in this way and it is the composite whole that matters, what about the composite whole of *Sunday In The Park With George*?

Finally, if time is a factor in that *Tosca* has been around long enough to have become 'great art', does this mean that *Oklahoma!* only has to wait 100 years for similar recognition? One is forced to remember the first production of *Madame Butterfly* at La Scala, Milan, on February 17, 1904 was 'a complete failure – one of the great fiascos of operatic history', according to Kobbe.

All this indicates that future sessions should allocate a great deal more time to nearly every one of the topics so quickly skirted in the session on 'producing in the musical theatre'. Only then can Cameron Mackintosh's unique contribution to academic development come to true fruition.

The programme for the Trinity Term is now available and includes sessions with performers, directors, composers and writers, all chaired by Mark Steyn.

Matching Musicals to Theatres

The Stage, 7 February 1991

On 15th February, 1951, Jack Hylton escorted Patricia Morison, Bill Johnson and Julie Wilson into the London Coliseum. They had arrived from New York to start rehearsals for *Kiss Me Kate*, Cole Porter's musical which was to take over the house occupied by *Annie Get Your Gun*.

The three New York stars took one look at the 2,354 seater and fled. They had come over to appear in this fairly intimate musical which had been playing in New York's New Century Theatre which seated 1,712 (it was demolished in 1962). Eventually *Kiss Me Kate* opened to enormous acclaim in London, although critics like Philip Hope-Wallace in The Guardian wrote: 'Although the chorus here is much larger than New York, the size of the Coliseum and the necessity to filter everything through microphones tends to slow down the pace of scenes dangerously'.

This wrong-headed policy of putting medium-scale American musicals into too-large houses in London was undoubtedly a combination of many factors. First, there was the need to meet the vast demand for American musicals to satisfy the British appetites whetted by the war years' deprivation: next there was the policy of American producers and creative teams to demand royalties far larger than we had been used to in Great Britain, and lastly there was the greed of British producers to cash in on the whole operation.

Thus *Oklahoma!* played in the St James Theatre (1,609 seats) in New York and to 2,283 seats in Drury Lane; *Annie Get Your Gun* in the Imperial Theatre in New York with 1,452 seats and the Coliseum with 2,354 seats; *Carousel* and *South Pacific* at the Majestic Theatre in New York (1,655 seats) and then Drury Lane (2,283 seats). Of course, seating capacity alone is not necessarily the only criterion but the ambience of large houses with a Circle, Upper Circle and Balcony seating over 2,000 obviously differs from a large house seating 1,600 seats in Stalls and Circle alone.

Some years or so ago I was asked by someone at an all-party meeting with the arts minister (then Norman St John Stevas) what books he could read about 'How to become an impresario' and I had to explain that I knew of none. However, I took him out for lunch and explained all that I knew about acquiring the rights of a play, contracts for artists, rentals of theatres and so on. However, one cannot teach enthusiasm, or pass on the taste and perception needed to be a producer, and, more than anything perhaps, the necessity to place the correct production in the right venue.

The texture of London theatres can only be assimilated over years of attending performances and Cameron Mackintosh has aptly described it in the recent South Bank Show as the casting of the right theatre being as important as casting the correct artists. Clarke Peters explained that Cameron, in transferring *Five Guys Named Moe* from Stratford East, went shopping for the right theatre as he goes shopping for a tie. Countless shows have failed primarily for being placed in the wrong venue, just as mediocre shows have survived in the right one.

Certainly the brilliant chamber opera *Sweeney Todd* was totally lost in the vast space of Drury Lane, although Sondheim's score has proved successful at Watford Palace and even at the Half Moon (120 seats).

The most important factor which drives right through the centre of this problem is one of finance. Theatre Projects launched Sondheim's *Company* at Her Majesty's Theatre (1,210 seats) in January 1972. Another wonderful score was composed around George Furth's book, not just about some Americans, nor even about some New Yorkers, but about a very narrow section of Manhattan society. The show ran for 37 weeks and lost 90 per cent of its capital even having had the benefit of Hal Prince's superb direction and the memorable performances of Elaine Stritch and Larry Kert. Recently, however, there was a brilliant production of *Company* launched at the Oldham Coliseum (576 seats) directed by Paul Kerryson. It would have been wonderful to have transferred it to the West End since London deserves to see *Company* again. The ideal theatre for this production would have been the Duchess (with 474 seats) but with a cast of 14 and four musicians it was impossible to make such a venture economically possible. Even in theatres seating up to 700 or 800 the finances simply would not work.

Currently, Century Theatre has very bravely launched a tour of *Company* with a cast of 14, of which 13 (that is everyone except the role of Robert) play the score (on saxophones, trumpets, violins, bass and alto and percussion). It is an imaginative and worthwhile venture although not up to a standard which could warrant a transfer to the West End. Undoubtedly compromises had to be made to reduce costs and make the show possible. This meant that when listening to the music one felt they were quite good musicians for performers and when watching the performances one had to make the concession that they were quite good for musicians.

Naturally in touring their productions, Century Theatre (and *Company* is playing in Horsham, Harlow, Poole, Rotherham and Bury St Edmunds in February alone) can hardly pick and choose the correct ambience in which to play – they cannot even choose their best and cheapest route when at the mercy of available dates. Producers are also often at the mercy of available theatres in London: so timing becomes a matter of crucial importance as well as a governing financial factor. Nowadays one may have to wait some years for the right artists for a play, the right director, the right designer, the right lighting designer as well as the right theatre. Obviously the size and ambience of the auditorium is vital to a production, but one also takes into account the atmosphere in which one will be working which is created by the manager and his staff. One can immediately feel the vibrations from artists about which theatre they like or hate and much depends on the efficiency of, and welcome they receive from, the manager. A good manager is worth his weight in gold to a landlord.

All this delay must be irritating to dramatists and composers. In the forties and fifties one could write a play and see it staged within three months of putting in the last full stop. Last year the Stephen Sondheim Master Classes at Oxford spawned workshop performances of a number of exciting musicals, seen by many would-be producers who might yet achieve their being launched in the West End in years to come. Thus, the following musicals might well have to be patient for some time.

Horatio by Denise Wharmby went some way to answer the demand for comedy in new musicals and artists from *Phantom, Miss Saigon* and *Les Misérables* which admirably sang the students' work to a remarkably high standard. This amusing send-up of oratorio-like arias was also superbly sung by an Australian opera singer on holiday here, David Hobson, who should be captured immediately by the London musical world.

Harvest Moon Rising by the talented Leslie Arden does for Canada what *Oklahoma!* did for the U.S. This was an exciting score and the audience was unexpectedly lifted out of their seats with songs called *On The Farm, Welcome to Canada, Jennie, He Said My Father Was A Farmer, This Is Going To Be The Best Day Ever* and *Dear God Thank You For The Blessings.*

Eyam by Andrew Peggie and Stephen Clark had an original setting in a Derbyshire village in 1665 whilst the Great Plague raged in London. This score included a beautifully melodic love-song in *Promise Me You'll Never Change.*

Yusupov by Kit Hesketh-Harvey and James McConnell dealt with the massacre at St Petersburg and was distinguished by a talented *Hold Your Breath* chorus and magnificent *Where I'm Going, You'll Never Know* sung with superb Dietrich-like quality by Michael Strassen.

But young producers need look no further for a really true musical comedy called *Maxie* by Stephen Keeling and Shaun McKenna (based on the film). The distinguished audience (including Sondheim, Lionel Bart, Peter Nichols and Cameron Mackintosh) hugged itself with glee at show-stopping numbers like *I've Got Time For You* and one which should be called *Second Chances Don't Often Come Around*.

Lack of space does not permit me to recount further achievements of last year but there was enough talent here to fill West End theatres for decades to come – always provided, of course, that the right show finds the appropriate house.

The Economics of the Orchestra

Paper delivered in Stockholm, November 1985 at the Conference on 'The future of the Symphony Orchestra'. The Editors are grateful to the Conference organiser for permission to publish Professor Field's paper.

In November 1985, the Swedish National European Music Year Committee organised a conference in Stockholm concerning 'The Future of the Symphony Orchestra'. The Committee's Chairman, Ake Holmquist, explained that: "In spite of differences in artistic and political ambitions in the field of culture, in financial and marketing methods and in the working conditions for both orchestral musicians and administration, symphony orchestras the world over are faced with enormous artistic, cultural and financial problems. The future role of the orchestras, both as a bearer of tradition and as a medium for new creativity is dependent on how these problems are solved."

In due course, the participants included representatives from Austria, Belgium, Denmark, Finland, France, West Germany, Italy, Holland, Norway, Portugal, Roumania, Spain, Switzerland, Czechoslovakia, Turkey and Sweden as well as the representatives from the United Kingdom. Japan, Canada and the United States also sent observers to this European Conference since they considered it a uniquely useful forum.

On the first day there were the formal opening addresses, including a welcome from the Deputy Prime Minister of Sweden, and, most suitable, some music played by young Swedish performers (piano, violin, 'cello and flute). There followed a three-hour session of papers and debate on 'The symphony orchestra – a creative medium?' led by Luca Lombardi (an Italian composer), Jan Morthenson (a Swedish composer) and Martin Jones (Chairman of the Philharmonic Orchestra). The debate, perhaps predictably, revolved around the problems of how best to present new music. Should contemporary music be isolated into special programmes or included in traditional programmes? On the one hand there was a body of opinion that felt strongly that it was unwise and unfair to expect 'traditional' audiences faithfully attending the regular Beethoven, Tchaikovsky, Mozart concerts to welcome readily a 'sandwich' programme with contemporary music as the filling! The opposite faction clearly considered that it was unwise to isolate the audience for contemporary music in a 'ghetto programme' leaving standard orchestra programming as hardly being creative. Certainly the feeling in Sweden was that the audience for new work was a totally new and different section of the population, more likely to be on the fringe of rock and pop than standard classical fare. The debate had to be curtailed so that we could attend a concert by the Swedish Radio Symphony Orchestra.

The concert proved to be a sandwich where the bread was Poulenc and Janacek and the filling was a first performance of a concerto for guitar and orchestra by Sven-David Sandstrom. This enormously difficult new work was presented, albeit to this special audience, with absolutely no advance preparation or explanation even by the composer who was present. Although I understand that there were special reasons for this, it was only yet another illustration of the way audiences are treated in relation to new music.

On the second day, there was an opening session on 'Repertoire responsibility and programme planning' led by Bengt Olof Engstrom. This was followed by speeches from West Germany on 'The symphony orchestra and new distribution media'. Naturally there was a senior executive from Polygram there with all the latest technological details. The general reaction was that no degree of perfection in recordings would result in replacement of the live symphony concert anymore than pictures had replaced the desire to travel. The third and final session on the second morning was on 'The economics of the orchestra', a debate led by an address by Anthony Field. His paper on this subject is published here in advance of the publication of all the papers delivered at the Conference.

The second day's luncheon reception was provided by the City of Stockholm in the splendid City Hall and that afternoon the participants split into seven working groups of up to 20 people in each group. Unfortunately, progress in the group discussions was impeded to a minor extent by the mix of official languages of English, French and German (since the groups were not aided by the simultaneous translation available in the main conference) and to a major extent by the fact that the working groups were all left individually to decide on what they wished to discuss. Thus, a great deal of time was taken up by arriving at the major interest of each group, hoping that it would not prove to be the same as all the other groups.

The second evening concert was given by the Stockholm Philharmonic Orchestra (works by Haydn and Allan Pettersson).

The final morning was given to 'The orchestra musicians of the future - education and working conditions'. Anna Lindal, the second concert master of the Stockholm Philharmonic Orchestra, gave a most telling exposition of the problems of being a young musician in a symphony orchestra today.

The conclusion of the conference was based on all the Group leaders reporting on the findings of each of the seven groups. Although there had been a number of individual proposals put to the conference only one appeared to be universally accepted and this was to move towards the formation of a European league of Symphony Orchestras.

The Association of British Orchestras was one of nine national orchestral associations from Europe and beyond represented at the Conference. After the conclusion of the Conference, these associations took advantage of the opportunity to exchange information on orchestral life in their various countries and the work of their associations.

It is essential to preface this paper with a note to the effect that the views expressed in it are personal to me. Although the theories which follow have evolved during three decades of work in arts administration, mainly as Finance Director of the Arts Council of Great Britain, they are in no way to be associated with any organisation or group of individuals in Great Britain.

Until early in the nineteenth century, music was composed and performed for any aristocrat who would employ a composer. It was the convention and fashion that music should be provided at social occasions. Hence, not only were new costumes expected, but also a new suite of music. Thus the consumption of music was roughly proportional to what was being composed since the music being performed as contemporaneous. In 1830 a significant event took place when Mendelssohn organised a performance of Bach's St. Matthew Passion. The fact that this music was then a hundred years old started a trend which still obtains. The result of this development led to the institutionalisation of the Symphony Orchestras as well as the problems now experienced by composers as outlined by Michael O'Hare, a Professor of Urban Studies at the Massachusetts Institute of Technology, in a paper to be delivered at the first international forum on arts and economics held in Edinburgh, Scotland in 1979. He raised there the question of why so many more writers make a living from their work than composers. The first factor is that literature has a shorter life span than music: for example, the music of the eighteenth century is commonly performed and widely appreciated, while there are few exceptions to the fact that the literature from that period is a specialised taste. It is an interesting question as to why the language of music seems to become more accessible with age, whilst the language of prose becomes less so. Another factor is the restriction of literature to a particular language. Michael O'Hare cites the case of "one population keeps twenty novels and twenty symphonies in use, two populations speaking different languages will support forty novels" – but only a few more than twenty symphonies.

The plight of modern composers is not a subject for which we have time in this particular analysis of orchestra economics, but it is certainly illustrative of the problems caused by institutionalisation. For decades whilst I was at the Arts Council I railed against the subsidised orchestras refusing to give an inch on the traditional concept of concert promotion: the lighting, the formal attire of the players, the arrival of the leader, the conductor and the soloist, the formation of the programme, even the length of performance all follow a prescribed pattern. The rare exceptions imposed during wartime restrictions were soon jettisoned in 1946. The occasional departure of 'Prom concerts' involve the informality of the audience, not the performers. The rare symphony 'pops' concert (an idea over a hundred years old in America) is still comparatively unknown in Europe; the juxtaposition of different styles of music such as jazz with symphonic music, being an occasional aberration for a fund-raising event or a charity evening.

An enormous breakthrough in the United Kingdom has been achieved by John Dankworth with the London Symphony Orchestra at the Barbican in August 1985 when seven widely different concerts played to capacity audiences. John Dankworth's programme stated that one should not know what to expect at a pops concert. "The formula can vary so much, and much of the music is heard for the first time. Moreover, a great deal of it, unlike a normal 'classical' concert is tailor-made for the orchestra and often specially produced for the night of the performance." John Dankworth continued by emphasising that the music at a good 'pops' concert is not lightweight but should be quality music, interestingly scored in a way that is rewarding to the listener and challenging to the orchestra. Thus we might well be returning to the early nineteenth century idea of new divertimentos or suites specially composed for the occasion!

But further, the recent L.S.O. Summer Pops included 'theatrical lighting' (the audience in comparative darkness, the lighting of the orchestra changing with the music and focusing attention on various sections of the orchestra), it included surprise guest artists as well as a conductor and soloists who introduced their music to the audience. Further still, the Musical Director and Conductor also played instruments (the saxophone and clarinet): and perhaps it was only this uniquely talented person that could bring about this achievement. However, I remember Sir John Barbirolli introducing the music of the Hallé Orchestra to school performances I attended in the 1940s but then education should not stop when one becomes an adult! And even before Barbirolli, there was Pachman who talked whilst he played his piano .....

This may all seem a long way from any discussion on the impact of modern economics on the orchestra, but I consider it essential for orchestras, their concerts and repertoire to be constantly changing, living and breathing, creative organisations rather than a section of the arts world which politicians confine under the heading 'Museums and Galleries'. It is essential for orchestras to remain, as performing organisations, within the section of the arts world containing drama companies, opera and dance companies and other truly creative forces.

However, the economics of an orchestra is obviously different from the other performing companies. True, the four broad headings of income are the same: the ticket sales, sponsorship and patronage, exploitation of product and subsidy. Let us quickly review these:

(i)   A study by Abdul Khakee and Goran Milsson on Music and Theatre in Sweden (also delivered in Edinburgh in 1979 and published in 'Economic Policy for the Arts' by Abi Books) indicated that orchestras, opera and drama companies appeared to be playing to approximately 80% of capacity. Further, "attendance at concerts is made up of a narrow segment of the Swedish population, about 3%". This is identical with similar statistics in other countries. Attempts to broaden the social composition of audiences is a social rather than an economic or artistic consideration, since it is unlikely to increase audiences .... indeed an increase to 4% of the population attending concerts would cause audiences in every concert-hall to overflow.

What I do find a cause for concern is the narrowing of the range of seat prices. In 1945 British concert prices ranged from an average of two shillings up to ten shillings. Thus the top price was about five times the lowest price and a move from one price to another was a serious consideration for a concertgoer. Current London programmes indicate *average* prices range from £5 to £10. Thus the top price is often about twice the lowest price. Indeed, where concerts are charging £5, £6, £7, £8, £9 and £10 a move from one seat price to another is of little consideration. The bottom prices are much too high; they discourage the lower-paid and the young married people (according to Baumol and Bowen, the non-ticket costs of transport, meals and drinks and baby-sitters account for 46% of the total cost of attending a performance: see 'The Performing Arts: The Economic Dilemma'). Further, the top prices are much too low ....

and if you disagree please stand in a box office and listen to the people who want "two good seats in the front-row of the terrace" - that is what they want, they have been conditioned by radio, records and television to the good visual and aural impact of a concert and the price is immaterial.

(ii)   Sponsorship is more fickle than patronage. It requires a 'commercial return' and therefore goes for the well-tried music that can draw near capacity audiences. The commercial firm wants to be associated with the prestigious and is usually deaf to the continued acknowledgment they would get from the sponsorship of a new work rather than the fact that the memory of their association with a Tchaikovsky concert ends that evening. The different tax laws of the various countries also help to make this a difficult area to cover in a relatively brief paper.

(iii)   Income from the exploitation of product comes from radio and television, records and tapes. Obviously the heart of this problem is the question of royalties and it continues to be a monstrous injustice that any government should need one iota of persuasion to impose a levy on blank tapes which even at a very small level would produce much of the earnings rightly due to the creative and performing artists. I have never met a single consumer who has raised any objection to the imposition of a small levy on blank tapes. The only objections appear to arise from the sheer laziness and incompetence of the politicians and bureaucrats. The fact that a really complex system would be needed to provide total justice to everyone concerned should no longer be used as an excuse to continue the present injustice by which creative and performed work is raped by so-called civilised communities.

(iv)   Subsidy from central and local government should be called 'investment'. The return to the various Government Treasuries for investment in the arts has once-and-for-all been proved to be far in excess of the investment. In Great Britain the Treasury collects VAT at 15% on all ticket sales, there is the income tax collected from everyone employed in the arts industry (who would otherwise be claiming social security as unemployed), there is the income from foreign tourists who consistently list 'music, theatre, opera, dance, museums and galleries' as one of the three main reasons for visiting our country, there is the income from our companies touring abroad and the benefits from royalties earned abroad by composers, dramatists, writers and choreographers over the years. I appreciate that we have been using the important arguments that subsidies are required to improve the 'quality of life' but politicians are not interested in such abstruse advantages as education and style and civilisation, they are interested in industry and commerce, in defence expenditure and finance .... I repeat that we must replace the word 'subsidy' with 'investment'.

The main difference between the orchestras and other performing companies is that orchestral expenses have none of the flexibility of the others. Firstly, you either have an orchestra or you don't. You cannot walk into a restaurant and order caviar and champagne and state you will not pay more than £1. Likewise, a government cannot say "let there be orchestras" and not pay the bill. With a drama company you might, in times of economic duress, cut the size of the company. But you cannot cut the size of an orchestra to that of a chamber orchestra or a string quartet and pretend you have a symphony orchestra! Further, a drama company can economise on sets and costumes which is not an economy available to an orchestra. Nor can an orchestra disband for six months in a year and realistically ever be expected to come together again and become the same orchestra, whereas a theatre director can certainly close a theatre for six months as an economy and then reopen it.

What orchestras do have in common with other performing companies is that the programmes have to be balanced as well as the books of account! The delicate meeting of minds of the Finance Director with the Musical Director (call them what you will) must produce music in the concert halls and in the till. This can only be achieved through a vibrant repertoire and a creatively planned series of concerts. These are the foundations on which the music of nations is based.

I am afraid I must end on another contentious note. I do believe that orchestras, like all good arts organisations, should be independent. In the wake of last night's interesting concert by the Swedish Radio Symphony Orchestra and in the knowledge that BBC Symphony Orchestra may well assassinate me on my return to Great Britain, I must state that I do not believe it is the responsibility of any radio, television or film company to employ directly an orchestra any more than they should employ permanently an opera, dance or drama company. Nor do I think it is the job of a subsidising body such as the Arts Council of Great Britain to run a concert hall, like Wigmore Hall, or an Art Gallery, as they have done the Hayward Gallery. The fact that such orchestras or galleries have achieved unique success does not erode the argument that such bodies cannot be seen as truly impartial in the distribution of funds and in the independence of the artists is that much eroded.

Like the Surprise Symphony, I hope I am permitted a number of last notes. I must emphasise that for the relatively small investment governments make in music they get not only a good financial return but they get music all the way – on radio, television, records, films .... in shops and offices, airports and lifts .... the return to any nation is immense .... a world without music is unthinkable.

8 THE ARTS COUNCIL

The Arts Council – an Overview

I fear it is too late to provide a constructive overview because the Arts Council of Great Britain was destroyed by the professional party politicians years ago. Because politicians came to realise that the arts live on and cannot be controlled or destroyed and that they outlive governments, even the very civilisations that produced them, they were determined to break down what they came to see as an increasingly powerful body of truth. They did this quite stealthily by first dividing it into a Scottish Arts Council, a Welsh Arts Council and the Arts Council England, and then later, by infiltrating the Regional Associations and demanding that the decision-making be delegated yet further to them. Thus, there is now no longer any central body of artists which can make any impression on the politicians, let alone the Treasury. I fear that this will also happen eventually to the BBC, robbing it of all creativity and independence.

Anyone interested in this history should read the Arts Council's Annual Reports from 1946 onwards. They provide a superb story of half a century of achievement and destruction. Certainly the earlier Reports contain some superb essays by eminent people such as Sir William Emrys-Williams.

However, the arts cannot be destroyed altogether because they represent the substance of faith; they are what we find again when the ruins are cleared away.

The issue of *The Stage* (November 15) proves to be most significant with its two articles, one looking to the past and the other looking to the future. The first was the thoughtful tribute by Ron Pember to the late Josephine Wilson (Lady Miles) and Lord Bernard Miles, and the second on Shaping Up to the Future, an interview with the Arts Council's Secretary General, Anthony Everitt. Like so many issues of *The Stage*, the items of news and the articles about current issues in the theatre, drama and television which appear ephemeral end up by tracing the real underlying history of what is happening in the arts and entertainment world.

What is particularly significant about these two articles is that the one about the achievements of Lord Bernard Miles is all about creativity – the dedicated work which generated and developed the talents of writers such as Sondheim and Stoppard, in fact the endless list which Ron Pember describes as the amazing Who's Who of writers, composers, directors, designers and actors. On the other hand, Everitt's phrases about delegating Arts Council clients including 'geographical locus in the region', 'local authority funding', 'performing base' and 'companies involved with touring'… nothing about creativity. In point of fact, the Arts Council's criteria were chosen, says Everitt, to rest on objective situations rather than subjective value judgments because "we would never stop arguing about them".

My dictionary defines 'subjective' as 'arising from the mind' and certainly Bernard Miles did not shrink from subjective judgments in choosing works by Moliere, O'Casey, Shaw, Shakespeare and an enterprising list of new plays over a period of 22 years.

From 1945 to 1985 the Arts Council chairmen and secretary-generals also did not avoid subjective decisions which led to the greatness of the British arts and entertainment industry as the world now knows it. Lord Keynes' work as the Arts Council's first chairman was taken up by Sir Ernest Pooley, then Sir Kenneth Clark, Lord Goodman, Lord Cottesloe and Sir Kenneth Robinson. There was a creative line of progression, every step of which could be charted as closely as Lord Clark's Civilisation series.

Likewise, the first secretary-general, May Glasgow, handed over to Sir William Emrys-Williams, then Nigel Abercrombie, Sir Hugh Willatt, Sir Roy Shaw –

another creative line of progression. There has been a similar identifiable contact with creativity in each deputy secretary-general, although last time I highlighted the past distinguished personalities on the Arts Council, its Advisory Panels and Senior staff, I was referred to by Ian Brown (the Council's drama director) writing in *The Stage* as best ignored in kind silence as part of 'golden ageism'.

It is always easy to point out that the great names from past Advisory Panels are easy to identify in retrospect. However, perhaps we could have identified for us the present individuals on the Council and its Advisory Panels who are revered by the various arts professions as were, in their time, past members. Just 20 years ago, the Drama Panel included JW Lambert, Constance Cummings, Peter Dews, Richard Findlater, Philip Hedley, Peter James, Hugh Jenkins, Oscar Lewenstein, Peter Nichols, Timothy O'Brien, Richard Pilbrow, Peter Shaffer, Donald Sinden and Carl Toms. Thirty years ago it included Wynyard Browne, John Bury, Richard Findlater, Robin Fox, Val Gielgud, Frank Hauser, Leo McKern, Val May, Yvonne Mitchell, Joan Plowright and John Whiting. Forty years ago it included Sir Bronson Albery, Peggy Ashcroft, Sir John Gielgud, Michael MacOwan, Sir Laurence Olivier, Tyrone Guthrie, Noel Coward, Benn Levy, Sir Ralph Richardson and Andre Van Gyseghem. No wonder these talents were courageous enough to make subjective value judgments.

What mattered then to the Arts Council was that it was nurturing and fostering a climate in which new drama, music, opera, dance, painting and sculpture could be generated.

All that mattered then was that the work should be created and produced. It was then entirely up to other forces to take up the work, exploit it, tour it, educate audiences, raise sponsorship, disseminate it – to do all the things which the Arts Council now tends to concentrate upon while neglecting the basic need to create the work in the first place.

What I suggest is now needed is for the Arts Council, together with regional bodies and local authorities, to draw up a list of the creative companies in drama, music, opera, dance and the visual arts which shall remain the responsibility of the Arts Council. There are probably about 60 or 70 of them, large and small and easily identifiable. These companies should be properly subsidised to do their job and should be assessed primarily for creativity. There are but a handful of people in Britain capable of serving on the Advisory Panels needed to make such an assessment.

The second list would be the clients who are predominantly 'service' companies, who wish primarily to provide audiences with their basic, regular arts and entertainment fare. There are about 1,000 of these companies, large and small, and they can be assessed by Regional Arts Boards and also properly subsidised to do their job. Their main criteria of assessment will be efficiency and management, production and box office success. There is a tremendous number of people – accountants, business managers, lawyers, etc. – in the regions capable of serving on such an Assessment Panel.

It is high time, after over half a century, that we stopped pussy footing around this problem. Everyone knows well enough which companies fall into which category, and there is no need to put up a smokescreen to blur the situation by citing the one new play produced by a 'service' company or the one commercial comedy included by a 'creative' company on occasion. There is simply no stigma in being in one category or another and we should put behind us the British snobbery on both sides of this fence. We have been fortunate to create an arts and entertainment industry which leads the world and no one should be allowed to destroy it by implementing the present folly of proposals.

Subsidy and the Commercial Theatre

The Stage, 27 January 2000

Readers of my pieces in *The Stage* over the past three decades will know how hard I tried to persuade the subsidised theatre to move towards the commercial theatre by generating more work for West End and Broadway exploitation; and likewise to move the commercial theatre towards accepting subsidised ideas such as the Half Price ticket booth and the Theatre Investment Fund.

Similarly, I have tried to help bring various theatrical forms closer together. The hitherto snobbishness of British theatre folk separately categorised into Opera, Ballet, Musicals, Operetta, Drama, Dance, Concerts, Musical Comedy, Rock Concerts and so on has also slowly succumbed to dance musicals like *Cats* (over forty years after George Balanchine left Diaghilev's *Ballets Russes* to choreograph *On Your Toes*), through-sung musicals like *Les Misérables* (also forty years after Ezio Pinza left the Metropolitan Opera to star in *South Pacific*) and shows even more difficult to categorise such as *The Hunting of the Snark*.

In the past year I have become aware that an increasing number of scripts, scores, tapes, videos and even just ideas have come to me which can by no means be classified as the usual rubbish which floods into every producer's office. However, they appear to be difficult to produce, exploit or market in any way because, sadly, London has no venue suitable for them.

I was first made aware of this when discussing a number of possible projects with Cameron Mackintosh some years ago. We both had enormous admiration for *The Hunting Of The Snark* but were convinced it was not right for a West End theatre. Many such problems go onto producers' shelves until they solve themselves, as did *Tell Me On A Sunday* and *Variations* when Cameron put them together into the enormously successful *Song and Dance*. In the end, Mike Batt decided to produce *Snark* at the Prince Edward remembering that Timothy O'Brien softened the harshness of this auditorium with his brilliant side-hangings for *Evita*. However, even the wonderful designs for *Snark* did not persuade the audience who might well have packed it out at Wembley Arena to set foot inside a West End theatre; and the West End audience who went to see a 'musical' at the Prince Edward wondered what on earth they had experienced! Similarly Cameron Mackintosh attempted to make the Piccadilly architecturally hospitable to *Moby Dick*, which sat so beautifully in the Fire Station at Oxford.

I was reminded of this when I received a promotion package for *Which Witch?*, complete with CD and video, and the producers have not put a foot wrong. With Kit Hesketh-Harvey they have an impeccable lyricist; Richard Hudson's sets are always dazzlingly inspired; Martin Koch has a superb musical pedigree; Mark Bailey's costumes add joy to any production, Peter Thompson is the most creative of press reps, and Dewynters could market 'Springtime For Hitler' into a hit! (Oh, I forgot it was a hit!)

But as we all know only too well, the end result in showbusiness bears no relationship to logic, reason, justice or fairness.

I have written before about finding the right show for the right theatre, but there is now a great deal of excellently created work which cannot properly fit into a West End theatre – neither the beautiful playhouses on Shaftesbury Avenue nor the wonderful opera houses of Covent Garden, Drury Lane or the Coliseum, nor Wembley Arena, Olympia or Earls Court, nor the intimate spaces of the Bush, King's Head, or Donmar Warehouse...

Sadly, London lacks some flexible spaces (Oh dear, there must be a better phrase than that). The Roundhouse once filled part of this gap, without which we have much less chance of seeing productions from Manchester Royal Exchange, Glasgow Citizens, Scarborough or Stoke on Trent's theatre in the round. The problem with such spaces as the Roundhouse is that they came on to the scene with excitement and flair and after a few years started to become routine. The more you 'improve' a space, the more inflexible it becomes. But apart from this kind of extraordinary space we also have no equivalent in London of New York's supper-rooms or jazz haunts other than the indefatigable Ronnie Scott's Club or Pizza on the Park's unique work. But these cannot take the money to support more than a jazz trio and singer, and certainly cannot technically stage a scripted show. Sadly, we have also lost such 'club theatres' as the Boltons, the New Lindsay, the Irving, the Watergate, the Embassy and the Q. We have also lost such larger suburban houses as Holborn Empire, Finsbury Park and Wood Green Empires, Chelsea Palace, Collins Music Hall, Kingston Empire and, no doubt, any moment now, Shepherd's Bush Empire and Golders Green Hippodrome.

One exciting innovation was when Theatre Projects moved *The Mysteries* from the 400 seat Cottesloe Theatre into the Lyceum where 800 people could be accommodated. Iain Mackintosh's courageous and imaginative flair saw the possibilities of using this dilapidated space for a short, successful season of

Mysteries at the Lyceum. Maybe someone should have had similar ideas for venues for Peter Brook's *Dream* and the RSC's *Nicholas Nickleby*, both of which would have been enhanced by the kind of inspired production of *Candide* in New York and, more recently, in Calgary. Occasionally a unique brainwave results in theatregoers flocking to the most unlikely venue as when Mark Watty's production of Stephen Sondheim's *The Frogs* was presented at Brentford Public Baths in July 1990.

Perhaps what is needed is a structured approach to a 'Theatre Squatters Company'. Many imaginative groups and productions could occupy empty factories, offices and showrooms for short seasons.

I also experienced a most exciting night in San Francisco when Cleo Laine, John Dankworth and the San Francisco Symphony Orchestra wowed 6,000 people who came with hampers of food and drinks into a large hall set out with long wooden tables and benches on a flat floor. The audience had its 'Glyndebourne-style' meal at 6.30 and then enjoyed two hours of good music in the carnival atmosphere evoked with hundreds of balloons bedecking the tables. London would be hard put to stage such a spectacle even in the Albert Hall and certainly not in the Barbican or Royal Festival Halls.

Well the gauntlet has been thrown down by the creative artists…composers like Mike Batt, lyricists like Kit Hesketh-Harvey, artists like Marion Montgomery, musicians like Alec Dankworth, lighting designers, dramatists, set designers, costume designers, sound designers and many, many dramatists are all crying out for new spaces in which to develop their ideas. There will always be plays and musicals for our 45 wonderful theatres in London but the creative artists and performers now need some new spaces in London.

My colleagues at Theatre Projects have attempted to solve these problems of flexible spaces in a range of theatres holding 400, 800 and 1,000 people in places such as Calgary, Baltimore, the Derngate at Northampton and the Cottesloe Theatre. These have all been enormously successful in their own individual ways.

These same colleagues are now being challenged by the new problems of the 21st century.

Building Jerusalem

Review by Anthony Field, Theatres Trust Newsletter, August 1999

John Pick and Malcolm Anderson have produced a book entitled *Building Jerusalem: Art, Industry and the British Millennium* [Publisher: Harwood Academic Publishers, 1999]; this time a major work which is indispensable reading for all arts administrators. Starting with the long history of Royal and Church patronage, elaborating industrial support for the arts, describing the various public lotteries commencing in 1567, listing special events from the Great Exhibition to the Festival of Britain, recording the creativity of radio and television and the media and finally denigrating the work of the Arts Council of Great Britain, this book achieves a most detailed account of Britain's cultural past.

Whole sections of this work should be compulsory reading for anyone working in the arts and entertainment world, since it is essential that cultural policy-making should never be divorced from cultural history. For its first forty years, the Arts Council carefully paid close heed to this history, but suddenly there was a disastrous break with the past which has led to our leisure industries approaching the millennium in a state of cultural confusion.

So often we receive reports of the mobile Americans who all appear to donate and subscribe funds to their local theatres, orchestras, opera and dance companies, but we cannot be reminded too often that for centuries in the UK public subscription schemes of various kinds developed everything from libraries to book clubs, theatres to orchestras and even cinema chains. Further, unlike the Millennium Dome's solitary presence in a London borough, the Great Exhibition in 1851 fostered similar schemes in Birmingham, Nottingham, Glasgow and Manchester. Indeed, Manchester's exhibition helped to develop the Hallé Orchestra from a small group working on a shoestring to an enlarged orchestra, firmly established and making annual profits of some £2,000.

Building Jerusalem has 300 pages packed with fascinating information and indisputable facts, peppered with a number of critical arguments we have come to expect from these two distinguished writers. The chapter on 'The Horrors of Tourism' quite correctly reflects the true horrors but ends by comparing figures for Britons' expenditure on overseas holidays with that spent by incoming tourists and includes the odd statement that, "because home admissions to arts events are priced so low, British people are enabled to spend more and more of their money on overseas holidays".

The chapter on 'The Mirage of the Millennium' is illuminating and emphasises that "we still do not know the purposes of this celebration". It is particularly startling when set alongside the chapter on 'The Great Exhibition' which explains that the Crystal Palace was larger than the Millennium Dome and was built more quickly!

The book maintains that it is a "monstrous untruth" that the arrival of the Arts Council meant that "the great mass of ordinary people were now making their first tentative contacts with music, drama and the visual arts". The authors cite the arts activities which previously flourished, such as, "West End theatre, Penguin paperback books, the commercial reps, the Carl Rosa Opera Company and Bertram Mills Circus". However, I fear that both then and now the arts and entertainment business, profession or industry (call it what you will) still only directly reaches less than 5% of our population.

The final chapter 'Shadows and Illusions' poses an enormous number of pertinent questions for us all. However, once again the authors are incited to move away from all their usual rational debates to present emotive arguments against such notions as 'charities'. Charities are non-profit distributing so it is hard to be persuaded by the authors accusing them of "enjoying relief of taxation exceeding £2 billion per year".

There is no explanation as to how this has been calculated, particularly as there are no 'profits' to be taxed in any case; and if there is a 'surplus' it has to be ploughed back into the business and not 'enjoyed' by any individuals. Similarly, it has always been difficult to understand criticism of impresarios who are supposed to cream off the profits so that they can wine and dine in the South of France. From C.B. Cochran to Cameron Mackintosh, history has shown that they simply go on ploughing their money back into the business and, like playing the Las Vegas one-armed bandits, eventually the money runs out …

I hope all this has whetted appetites to go out and buy *Building Jerusalem*. The title belies the fact that this is really an invaluable volume for all readers of the Theatre Trust's Newsletter (and many others).

Politicians and the Pot of Gold

Tony's 1985 article is an impassioned assault on both the Arts Council and, more importantly, politicians, and how the arts are treated. His basic point is that investment in the arts is not just civilised and admirable in itself – it also makes money for the economy as a whole and is thus commercially sensible.

As the tone and content of the piece suggests, this fact is greeted with cold incomprehension at best – and a perverse refusal to hear home truths at worst – by the powers-that-be. Tony refers to this being the case for 30 years: it has also been the case in the 20 or so years since the article was first published.

His insistence that the regions are best administered and aided by people in the regions, rather than a centralised body, will strike a chord with early 21st century readers who have seen the present (at time of writing) government create an ever more unwieldy and intrusive bureaucracy, despite the establishment of some high-profile devolved bodies, especially in Scotland and Wales.

His last sentence will raise some eyebrows (how could civilisation continue, in a major way, in the immediate aftermath of a nuclear attack?) and it could be argued that his anti-political point could have been made better by saying politicians didn't care about civilisation as they didn't particularly expect it to survive in any case. The article is clearly written in the Cold War context of potential nuclear war at any given moment, but it also has a contemporary resonance: Michael Portillo, generally accepted to be perhaps the most arts-orientated Member of Parliament of his generation (though Gerald Kaufman might take umbrage at that) is leaving Westminster to pursue his career in the arts – including his position as theatre critic for (improbably enough) the New Statesman.

Tony's comment about *Cats* in the penultimate paragraph is also well made: many a theatrical ship has been sunk for the want of a ha'penth worth of tar, or has failed even to get down the ramp and into the water: a state of affairs that sends playwrights and composers into despair but also loses people employment, theatres their customers and the tax man his revenues on theatre profits, salaries, etc. Raising money in a notoriously risky business continues to be one of the most pressing problems facing young writers and producers.

Tony's championing of the subsidised sector is understandable, though Andrew Lloyd Webber, writing recently in *The Stage*, argued the other way – that subsidised theatre was undermining rather than supporting the commercial sector, as commercial producers couldn't compete with the subsidised/ sponsored low prices that the National Theatre (for example, with its Travelex

£10 seasons) was able to offer. The debate, clearly, has two sides to it and will continue to arouse strong feelings, with both sides having some justification to their arguments. Nick Hytner, at a National Theatre press conference, said the commercial theatre wasn't any concern of the National, but the two sectors have an enormous amount in common and mutual cross-over, so their relationship will always be the subject of discussion by people in the industry.
PW

The Pot of Gold at the end of a Subsidised Rainbow

The Guardian, 8 March 1985

To most people working in the arts and entertainments industry, the last few months of debate appear to have been more destructive than constructive. Effort and time are wasted when one art form rails against another, or when yet another useless lobby or rally is convened to indict a political party or attempt to draw attention to the fact that a five per cent uplift in subsidies would make all the difference to the development of an industry which employs 594,000 people (against the level employed in motor vehicle manufacturing).

In my last few years at the Arts Council we spent a lot of time producing statistics which proved conclusively that subsidies to the arts and entertainment were a lucrative investment for any government. When we were also able to show that a further £5 million invested in the Arts Council would bring in extra revenue of £15 million, civil servants would look to their shoes, mumble acquiescence and turn to another page of estimates.

Thirty years ago, when the arts industry had a few amateur administrators, it was simple for a civil servant to look at a request for £1.3 million from the Arts Council, consider this to be artificially inflated and respond with a £1.1 Million grant.

Since then, professional training of arts administrators has developed at the City University to such an extent that the detailed estimates compiled from those prepared by more than 1,000 organisations are tried and tested and tempered to reach the exact minimum amount required to sustain the industry. So, who are the Treasury officials who consider these estimates can be ignored and that a two per cent uplift is sufficient to sustain the present return of £300 million to the Treasury for the £100 million grant to the Arts Council?

The argument to replace government subsidy with sponsorship generated by tax incentives is a separate matter. Even in the USA it has been conceded that a centrally planned approach to the distribution of arts subsidies is a better method than haphazard tax concessions being picked up by commercial firms: sponsorship is governed by almost every consideration other than the planned development of an arts administration.

The American entertainments industry has undoubtedly suffered from the lack of a Royal Opera, Royal Ballet, Royal Shakespeare or National Theatre company. These can only grow out of regular annual subsidy. Americans are coming to realise that it is only by giving opportunities to a permanent group of creative artists that experiments like *Educating Rita* and *Piaf* evolved in a studio theatre can end up as hit shows in the West End and on Broadway.

In such ways one can compile the achievements and calculate the return to the Treasury. Leonard Bernstein recently visited this country to see the current production of his *West Side Story* and was overwhelmed by the tremendous professionalism and zest of the British cast.

The recent achievements in British Theatre are all based on the regular investment in subsidised companies since the inception of the Arts Council in 1946. The biographies of every writer, director, designer, actor, dancer, singer, choreographer, musician and composer in the programmes of every West End show are peppered with work and training in subsidised companies.

Let us stop mincing words: there would be no radio, no television, no magazines, no cinema, no commercial theatre, no entertainment in the country without the initial investment of government subsidy.

So what is the return to the Treasury? Firstly and quite simply, the VAT on admission tickets. *Cats* would not have evolved were it not for Trevor Nunn's experience gained at the RSC and the dancers involved who were trained by our leading ballet companies. The VAT collected by the Treasury on *Cats* in London now amounts to £3 million, and the advance bookings on the three American productions at present total £8.5 million.

Which brings me to the second important return to this country – the income from our arts exports. It is increasingly sickening to creative artists to watch governments bask in the glory of achievements such as *Gandhi* and *The Killing Fields*, television programmes from *Upstairs Downstairs* to *Jewel In The Crown*, our orchestras touring abroad, The English National and Covent Garden companies' recent successes in the U.S., our plays on Broadway (*The Real Thing*, *Noises Off*, *Nicholas Nickleby*), and our dance companies.

But governments' reward for the vast profits reaped is not increased investment but an occasional knighthood. Thus the few hundred pounds invested all those years ago in Joan Littlewood's *Oh What A Lovely War*, which started Richard Attenborough's career as a film director and led to his present role as director of *Chorus Line*, is repaid with a knighthood for him and not the extra £30,000 which is the life blood of the company at the Theatre Royal, Stratford East.

But the arts and entertainments industry cannot stand still: it develops or withers. So, quite apart from a 10 per cent work uplift to sustain the work of the existing companies the Arts Council needs a further £10 million for development work in the regions, not by moving money from London, but by proving conclusively to the Treasury that such investment will bring a return.

How could it be spent to maximum effect? I believe that the Arts Council should decide exactly which regional companies have the strongest administrative and financial boards and channel regional monies in those directions. The hundreds of local people who have given their time and experience to working on boards of management, in many cases for a great many years, form one of the best bases for such developments.

For example, the Hallé Orchestra might be chosen to pioneer the development of music-making in the Northwest; the Exeter Northcott Theatre might be chosen to spearhead the provision of drama in the southwest. The administrative and financial structures are there already.

With small amounts of extra support the main boards of management throughout the regions can shoulder more responsibility: the orchestras can develop music-making from the small-scale touring of chamber groups to buying in jazz outfits; the major drama companies can develop small-scale touring from their own companies and extend the range of their programmes by providing bases for exciting small touring groups.

This can all be developed by the regional companies, who are already in active production and who know their areas better than any central body in Piccadilly. Only through a radical new approach to the distribution of funds, coupled with a change in how show business is allowed to develop its own programmes, can a new future be evolved and the present economic stupidity overcome.

However, the real tragedy is not the economic stupidity of governments or the blindness of their economic advisers (and I am talking about all our governments over the past 30 years since this is not really a political matter) but the failure of those who are supposed to lead this country to do so.

If they are not prepared to invest that 10 per cent more in the one industry which is really thriving, and if they are also not prepared to offer tax incentives to prospective sponsors, then they might turn their attention to tax incentives to individuals and organisations who are willing to invest in the entertainments industry. They might also apply their intelligence to dealing with the lack of interest in the City and banking institutions in the entertainments industry.

Since moving from the Arts Council back to the commercial theatre world I have been increasingly appalled by the attitudes of some within the banking profession towards the entertainment industry. The City's attention is confined to the property investment side of theatre and cinema, where millions of pounds of profit are creamed off the industry by evading and avoiding every conceivable conservation order, while a successful *Cats* or *West Side Story* might almost not have happened for want of £10,000. Slowly the Americans are coming to realise what creative talent is housed in Britain and the brain drain of the Fifties is becoming the fame drain of the Eighties.

The reason the arts and entertainment industry has been treated so shabbily over the years is because politicians are not interested in civilisation. No doubt because they know that civilisation will continue after they have blasted us all to pieces.

9 LECTURES

Commitment and Responsibility Recalled

Commitment and Responsibility was the title of my Alport lecture, given at the City University on 28 November 1983, to mark my Professorship there. Re-reading it after nearly two decades brings home to me that we have sadly lost a number of brilliant people to whom I refer, like Joseph Papp and Michael Bennett, and that others have gone on to achieve even greater success, like David Hockney and Cameron Mackintosh.

It also illustrates how many principles of British government funding still need to be scrutinised and how much we can continue to mistrust the word of professional party politicians who can make 'dishonest men' of us all.

I am also reminded of the responsibilities of the giver and the taker. The horrendous 'cash limits' system appears to have been devised by politicians who wanted to abrogate all responsibility for the consequences of funding. This was like the early years when the Arts Council would in effect say to a company: "You asked for £20,000, here is £15,000, now go away and perform". And if the company came back at the end of the year and said, "Well, the programme did cost £20,000, and we have a deficit of £5,000" or, worse still, "We cut our programme by 25% to work within the funds you gave us" – then that company was for the chop. After my appointment as Finance Director I soon realised that, as the funding body, we had a responsibility to work with each performing company to reach agreement on what could be achieved within available funds.

We have not progressed! As the Chair of Liverpool Institute For Performing Arts Ltd. we were told by the Higher Education Funding Council (HEFC) what funds were available and what we had to achieve. The government abrogates all responsibility as to whether the funds are adequate or whether the achievements are feasible. This is not 'government'…

Commitment and Responsibility

On 29 November 1983, Professor Anthony Field CBE, Finance Director of the Arts Council of Great Britain, delivered the 5th Alport Lecture at the City University.

When the first Alport Lecturer, Kenneth Robinson, spoke on the work of the Arts Council, he entitled his talk 'Support for the Arts Council – the Next Five Years'. He was, on the whole, able to paint a fairly hopeful picture, but he suggested that, in prudence, it would be wise to look again at the position of the Council soon after his five year period had elapsed. In a sense, this paper tonight is in response to his suggestion.

The first Annual Report of the Arts Council of Great Britain carried an Introduction to explain that on 12 June 1945, the Chancellor of the Exchequer announced in the House of Commons that the Council for the Encouragement of Music and the Arts (CEMA) would continue as a permanent organisation with the title 'Arts Council of Great Britain'. He said that it would be incorporated as an autonomous body and receive grant-in-aid direct from the Treasury.

On 9th August 1946, the Council was granted a Royal Charter and was offered a grant-in-aid of £350,000 for the year commencing 1st April 1946, and the Annual Report for 1946-47 included as an Appendix the conditions of the Agreement of the Council entered into with its clients. This Standard Agreement was 'to be signed by both parties and the conditions are binding and comprehensive'.

By the time this first Annual Report was published Lord Keynes had died, suddenly on Easter Sunday 1946, but his far-sighted imagination, vision and enthusiasm had laid the foundations for the Arts Council's work. He had written: "The day is not far off when the Economic Problem will take the back seat where it belongs, and the arena of the heart and head will be occupied, or reoccupied, by our real problems – the problems of life and of human relations, of creation and behaviour and religion".

In the thirty-eight years of the Council's history it has evolved a practice of work and developed a relationship with its hundreds of clients that is the envy of the world.

This paper is not the forum in which to debate yet again the freedom enjoyed by the arts whereby creativity is unencumbered by the controls elsewhere imposed by Government or implied by commercial support. Suffice to record that there has always been a gentleman's agreement with successive governments that the Council's Grant-in-Aid should be offered for a year's work and be sacrosanct. After all, "civilisation advances by extending the number of important operations which we can perform without thinking of them" (Alfred North-Whitehead) and the number of activities we can progress without regularly re-questioning them. Thus, the understanding from the outset was that the Council:

(a) Would be offered an outright Grant-in-Aid; that is, it would be non-returnable and any unspent balance would be carried forward at the end of one financial year into the next;

(b) Would keep normal double-entry books of account; that is, on a commitments basis and not on the Government's cash basis; and

(c) Supplementary grants would only be available in three events:

    (i)   The imposition of new legislation which levied additional costs on the arts (e.g. the introduction of VAT in 1973 with 10% on ticket sales reduced to 8% in 1974 and increased to 15% in 1979).

    (ii)   The impact of national or international affairs on arts finances (e.g. the outbreak of war).

    (iii)   The requirements on the Arts Council to undertake additional responsibilities (e.g. The Festival of Britain).

From its earliest years, the Council developed a special relationship with the government on the one hand and with its clients on the other. This relationship is very largely dependent on the avenue of communication which has been developed through the Assessorship system. Thus, the government has an Assessor (from the Office of Arts and Libraries) sitting on the Council as a non-voting presence at meetings. Similarly, the Council appoints an Assessor to each and every client in receipt of annual revenue subsidies. These are invariably the relevant subject Directors (attending Royal Opera House Board meetings with me) who often have to send an officer to represent the Council since Directors cannot attend the hundreds of meetings of all the clients.

The Assessorship system is an enormously constructive avenue of communications to help overcome such practical problems as those resulting from the system of annual subsidies. Quite often, too much has been made of the limitations of annual subsidies, although there are some very valid arguments in favour of a 'rolling triennium' system of arts funding. However, it has not really been true to pretend that an Arts Council client can be wholly ignorant of the level of available grant-aid to be made available for a subsequent year commencing on 1st April. There has always been an understanding that the Council's grant-in-aid and, in consequence, the Council's level of subsidy to its regular annual revenue clients, would not be less than in the preceding year, usually with an increase for inflation. There may well have been a debate about the index for the country as a whole. Certainly there would be an area of negotiation in respect of any extension of a company's work. However, a 'gentleman's agreement' has existed to cover any radical alteration of the level of Council subsidy which would be notified to the client, certainly six months and possibly twelve months in advance.

In practice, a great deal depends on the working relationship between the Government and the Council, the Council and the Boards of companies, through the presence of the relevant assessors.

Just as any experienced Finance Director keeps in a bottom drawer financial plans for the next three to five years, adjusting and amending them according to the dreams and aspirations of Boards and their Artistic Directors, so assessors keep a wary eye on Councils and Boards. This means that the O.A.L. Assessor can keep reminding the Council whether or not its expressed hopes and broad policy indications are going to be viable in terms of future Government fiscal policy or not. Further, the Assessor can report back to Government the Council's debates on priorities and can attempt to find ways of meeting the Council's need to respond to developing areas of the arts, at the same time as warning Government of the consequences of such developments if they are to result in restricted funds in other areas of work or regions of the country. This means that the Council and the Government can both be helped, particularly if arts development is running alongside other lines of national policy.

Such advantages are also gained by the practice of placing the Council's assessors on Boards of its clients whereby the Council can be warned of new developments, changing priorities and expected crises and the Company can be helped by an initial response, however informal, from its Assessor.

In other ways, the Council has also been helped by its contact with Government: the regular meetings of the Chairman with the Minister; and senior officers of the relevant Government Department (the Treasury, DES, OAL in recent years) with those of the Council. Particularly in the Autumn months these regular contacts have given each an opportunity to develop arguments about priorities. Government can ask: "What difference would another £1 million make?" and Council can affirm: "Without that £1 million the following activities would cease". Only through such negotiations which in no way erode the Council's autonomy, can the final figure be reached. The importance of such negotiations in terms of time cannot be stressed too strongly.

It is often necessary for Council to say to Government: "Without confirmation of that extra £1 million, the tour planned to start in April will have to be abandoned". Companies are, in turn, saying it to Council. And all down the line the wheels of decision-making and actual activity can only be oiled by this trust and understanding – the nods or shakes from officials to officials long before the formal exchanges of letters and pieces of legislation are actually in train.

To understand the enormous dilemma which faced the Arts Council in the current financial year, it is necessary to explain the ramifications of the system which has evolved over the past three decades. Once the Council had agreed how it intends to allocate its grant-in-aid, letters of intimation are sent to all its regular annual clients setting out what funds are to be made available in response to each application. Clients are then requested to revise estimates, programmes and plans to show how they intend to work within available funds. Only when these are received and agreed are formal offers sent setting out the details of grants and guarantees against loss together with the Council's conditions of financial assistance. Clients are required to complete a formal acceptance of the conditions of financial assistance.

The Council has always considered that its offers, the acceptances and the binding conditions together formed a formal contract, the consideration being on the one hand the Council paying the subsidies offered and, on the other, the product presented by the performing organisations. If the recipients broke the conditions of financial assistance the subsidies offered might be withdrawn or reduced. For example, if fewer productions or shorter seasons are presented. Similarly, it was considered that the commitments entered into by the Council's clients (e.g. contracts negotiated with artists, scenery and costumes ordered, programmes, playbills and exhibition catalogues printed, etc.) would, being dependent on the Council's formal offer, be met because the Council would honour its commitments.

It is true that once, before the Council's cash had been reduced, and this was when the incoming Conservative Government in June 1979 cut the cash grant of £60,375,000 which had been offered to the Council by the outgoing Labour Government, to £59,261,000. The Parliamentary Estimates had included the Council's commitment grant-in-aid at £63,125,000 on the basis of the cash available. The cash cut was made after the subsidies for the year 1979/80 had been intimated (and in many cases offered) and the Council decided to honour those commitments and to persuade Government to confirm its commitment Grant-in-Aid at the same figure (£63,125,000) on the understanding that the Council would control its cash expenditure within a lower figure of £59,261.000.

Although the original cash cut was £1,114,000, because of changes made in the cash payments to the Council during the year, the Council started the following financial year 1980/81 with a level of commitments brought forward £292,000 higher than had been planned.

This inevitably resulted in the following year's cash being already spoken for to the turn of £6,404,000 instead of £5,475,000 as had been planned. Thus the level of the commitment Grant-in-Aid in 1980/81 had to be fixed at £70,970,000 instead of £71,899,000 as otherwise might have been possible.

Certainly the media, let alone the public, never fully grasped this problem and very few people appeared to understand the arithmetic, as has been sadly demonstrated by the recent exchange of letters in *The Guardian* between Norman St. John Stevas and Sir Roy Shaw. None of these letters (no doubt because newspapers do not enjoy the space this paper can) fully dealt with the fact that a cut is a cut, and whilst Norman St. John Stevas was correct in the implication that the Arts Council had absorbed the cut without harming clients in the year in which it was imposed, certainly the full impact of it was felt by client in the ensuing year because it had to meet those it had necessarily carried forward from the preceding year. However incomprehensible the operation had proved to be, at least the Council had met its responsibilities; it had honoured its commitments and given its clients time to replan at a lower figure than they might otherwise have had intimated for the following year.

The situation facing the Council in 1983/84 was a little different. The 1983/84 level of grant-in-aid had been announced. The Government announced the cut in the cash grant in July 1983. Thus a reduction of 1% coming well into the financial year meant a reduction of almost 2% on the planned expenditure for the remainder of the year. The Council complained strongly to the Government that over-expenditure by certain Civil Service Departments should result in those Departments being cut and not on the cut being imposed on autonomous bodies like the Arts Council which has for 35 years worked within available funds. Further, it was demonstrated to the Treasury that the cut of nearly £1 million would lose the Treasury far more than that.

Arts Council subsidies generate monies from the box office, local authorities, industry and commerce and exploitation earnings (radio, television, video, film, tape and magazine income, etc.) at home and abroad – all of which is taxed by both Customs and Excise and the Inland Revenue. Such investment is lost forever and the country undoubtedly suffers; but that is another subject.

In the circumstances, the Arts Council had three options open to it:

1.   To do what it did in 1978/79 and honour its commitments to clients so that its clients in turn could behave honourable with their creditors. This had, however, three disadvantages:

   (i)   It would effectively exculpate the government and leave the Council in the position it faced in 1979/80 of having to explain why its clients could not receive the full benefit of the money available in the ensuing years.

   (ii) The published Government figures for the arts in 1984/85 were not so bright as to lead the Council to consider that it could so easily depend on an increased grant-in-aid sufficient to absorb the cut brought forward from the previous year and give clients any reasonable increase; and

   (iii) The cash flow situation of the Council and its clients was, for many reasons, so much tighter than hitherto that it was less able to maintain it commitment grant lever and operate with nearly £1 million less cash.

2.   Simply to cut all allocations by 1% including all offers of subside already made and accepted. The Council would have to plead *force majeure*. The advantage of this proposal was that it would bring home publicly where the responsibility lay for the cuts and would be a very clear way of dealing with the immediate situation. The disadvantages were that the Council could be sued for breach of contract and that where clients were already experiencing difficulties in maintaining an adequate programme on meagre resources the effect would be even more damaging.

3.   To attempt to absorb the cut without passing it on to annual revenue clients. This might have meant cutting the Council's own controllable activities which are nearly all in the Art and Literature fields. This has been done on a number of previous occasions when the Council has been attempting to balance its budgets. It is always tempting to cut Awards, Bursaries and prizes, the Council's exhibition activities, Arts Films, schemes such as Works of Art for Public Buildings, Photography, etc. This always benefits Drama, Music and Dance Allocations. It also would have meant cleaning out every conceivable balance in the Council's coffers – leaving the Council impotent for the remaining eight months of the year, depriving it of any room whatsoever to manoeuvre flexibly and productively.

In the event, although it was recognised by Directors and Council members that to honour its commitments was the constitutionally correct thing to do, the Council opted for the 1% cut across-the-board. One Council member is reported as saying that, "politicians are making dishonest men of us all".

As a result of this decision, letters were sent to all the Council's regular annual revenue clients withdrawing 1% of the total offer made and accepted earlier in the financial year. Since these letters were only sent out in late July and it was unlikely that Boards could act upon them until the second half of the financial year, the cut was, as Council had warned the Minister, more nearly 2% on the balance of the year. All the Council's allocations were correspondingly cut by 1% so events which had not yet been in receipt of an offer one way or the other suffered a similar fate.

There was never any question of the Council not applying the 1% across the board, once it was realised that the cut had had to be enforced. The £1 million of cuts in 1980 which led to the axing of subsidies to 41 companies was done as part of the Council's assessment process before the start of the financial year in question. In July 1983 the cut was imposed some six months after the entire assessment process had been completed; thus, cutting of the £93.5 million cake had to become the basis of the cutting of the £92.58 million cake. One cannot argue that what is an equitable division in January has become inequitable in July. Of course, had one started by assessing subsidies on a £92,58 million basis at the outset the result may have been quite different, but it is not possible to implement such an exercise well into a financial year.

The argument already foreshadowed by the Council was repeated – the Government departments which had overspent should be the ones to suffer the cut and not the innocent sectors which were successfully working within available funds. Indeed Dennis Healey, when Chancellor of the Exchequer, was so impressed with the Council's successful control of its commitments of over £686 million during its history that he attempted to move the Treasury towards similar controls to replace to stop-go lurching of its primitive cash-flow system whereby each summer's cuts are following by the inevitable cash hand-out bonanzas in the following March when, lo and behold!, the Treasury finds that increased wages have produced increased income from taxes and that the lack of control systems of commitments has resulted in lower than expected cash expenditure. But this is not the forum in which to explore the Treasury's inability to adopt for the country even the shadow of a proper system of controls which any professional accountant would install in the smallest arts centre. Indeed the recent White Paper on Stage One of the Government's financial management initiative has led to the Government being committed to doubling the number of professionally qualified accountants it employs within the next ten years. However, this month has seen the Government failing to attract a successor to Sir Kenneth Sharp, who has retired as head of the government accounting scheme.

Whatever the arguments about the effects of the 1% cut, the organisations affected had to look in turn to their own commitments. As these were largely organisations already bereft of reserves and working capital, many with a contingencies figure too small to absorb a 1% cut in subsidy, the only course available was to cut activities: touring weeks, the size of casts, the number of rehearsals, all the obvious options. The usual arguments have also been repeated in this area of work in that the larger organisations usually are committed to the longer-term plans. And particularly in the international field the costs involved in cancelling contracts are often greater than having to fulfil them. I am told by legal colleagues that this area of case-law is not very productive of precedents. The case of Tsakiroglou and Co. Ltd. vs Noblee and Thorl dealt with a shipper who contracted to take ground nuts from Port Sudan to Hamburg via the Suez Canal and who would have gone bankrupt had he taken the goods round South Africa when the Suez Canal was shut. Although the shipper pleaded *force majeure*, it was held that the contract should have been completed. This finding might not establish a legal basis on which subsidised companies could simply renege on their international commitments.

However, Theatre Workshop Limited has apparently been exploring the possibility of suing the Arts Council for breach of contract in not meeting the commitment undertaken in what have been considered contracts for over 35 years.

I am not a lawyer and I do not intend to explore what might be interesting legal analyses which could well be taken through many Courts and ultimately be dealt with in the House of Lords. It is hard to see who would gain by all this, even if the costs are raised from outside sponsorship. (The actors' union, Equity, had already indicated that it would be prepared to find monies towards such costs) since government funds cannot be used to take legal action against what is, in effect, the government. It could further be argued that such sponsorship funds could otherwise be used for arts activities anyway. The outcome of such a case would be not only to establish whether a contract exists between the Arts Council and its clients but also whether any contract exists between the Government and the Arts Council. There are a very few cases which impinge on this principle. The Australian Woollen Mills Limited vs the Commonwealth of Australia (1955) tried to establish unsuccessfully whether the Australian Government should honour its subsidy commitment to sheep-shearers and Rederiaktiebolaget Amphitrite vs Rex (1921) found that although the British Government had entered into an undertaking with the Swedish Government, which was neutral during the First World War, not to impound any of its ships, it immediately did so when a Swedish ship S.S. Amphitrite entered the port of Methil in the Forth (Scotland). In this case the Crown submitted that letters did not constitute a contract, and, further, that letters from the British Legation were expressions of the present intention of the Government and no more. It is difficult to see what good could come to the Arts Council, let alone the Atomic Energy Authority, the Milk Marketing Board, the British Council, and so on, if the law were to prove that since the Government is a law unto itself it does not have to honour any commitment from one day to the next.

This may well be acceptable when the business and commercial world knows that it is eating at the same table as the Government, even if being spoon-fed. But when successive Governments have over a period of a quarter or half a century, gone out of their way to maintain, by means of Royal Charter, charitable status, independent companies, etc., that they will respect the autonomy of such bodies, and acknowledge the arm's length of every spoon's length principle, it ill behoves them to renege on commitments.

This is where financial and legal commitment ends and human responsibility begins. The British temperament has developed and supported the 'gentleman's agreement' basis of working in many fields of activity. In the Stock Exchange a man's handshake is his bond; in the theatre world an oral promise to invest in a commercial production has been sufficient for any member of the Society of West End Theatre; in the auction rooms a nod of the head (or even a twitch of the ear) can be honoured later by the exchange of millions of pounds. The arts world has proved to be honourable. It has given back to the nation many millions of pounds more each year than the nation has chosen to invest in it. It has done this at the expense of the creative artists who spend their lives writing plays, composing music, choreographing ballets, directing operas; the performing artists who, when working, generally earn much less than the national average wage; and the arts administrators who have to work all day to balance the books and usually every evening when the theatres, concerts halls, dance and opera houses and arts centres are open.

The various returns to the nation from its modest investment in the arts have been investigated too many times with particular emphasis on the returns from Tourism into Great Britain and from the export of our arts all over the world. There are two particular returns which are even more dependent upon the Government's bond being kept. Firstly, the development of the inter-relationship between the subsidised and the commercial arts worlds which in the visual arts, dance, drama, music and literature is evolving rapidly in many directions. Whether it is the original Arts Council recognition of David Hockney, the commercial exploitation of his work in the film *The Bigger Splash* or the recent use of his designs in the Royal Opera/Royal Ballet double-bill of Ravel and Stravinsky, or whether it is manifested in Cameron Mackintosh's London productions of *My Fair Lady* and *Oklahoma!* after their Leicester Haymarket productions and Arts Council tours, we have all benefited. Maybe it can be seen in the use and development of the talents of Royal Ballet dancers in *Cats* and *Song and Dance*, coming thirty years after Broadway had shown us how to use Metropolitan Opera's Ezio Pinza in *South Pacific* and Robert Weede in *The Most Happy Fella* and forty-five years after using ballerina Vera Zorina in *I Married an Angel*. In New York last month at the end of the 3,389th performance of *A Chorus Line*, making it the longest running Broadway show ever, Joseph Papp and Michael Bennett embraced. This was not just show business sentimentality. Mr Bennett is the foremost director in the musical theatre; Mr Papp is the foremost producer in the non-profit theatre: these men work on the opposite sides of the American arts world. Yet neither Mr Bennett's career no Mr Papp's Public Theatre might now be thriving if Mr Papp had not given Mr Bennett a home in which to develop *A Chorus Line* a decade ago. When these two men embraced it was the most palpable reminder that the best people in the arts, commercial and subsidised, share a common bond and goal.

The second return to government is through the effect the arts can have on many areas of commerce and industry. Professor Galbraith, in his W.E. Williams Memorial Lecture in January, cited Italy as one of the miracles of modern industrial achievement with one of the highest rates of economic growth of any country in the western industrial world. He went on: "No one has cited in explanation the superiority of Italian engineering or science; or of industrial management; or the precision of Italian government policy and administration; or the discipline and co-cooperativeness of the Italian unions and labour force.

Italy has been an economic success over the last thirty-five years because its products look better – because Italian design is better".

I might add that my parents presented me with a portable Olivetti typewriter when I qualified as an accountant and it was, therefore, somewhat chastening to find that model in the Arts Council's Hayward Gallery Exhibition of 'Art and Design in the Thirties'. Italian design reflects the superb commitment of Italy to artistic excellence extending over the centuries. Professor Galbraith ventured that "no one is really qualified to become the head of an American automobile company these days unless he has an Italian name ... No British government would have dreamed of financing Mr De Lorean had his name been Jones or Smith.

The really important message from Professor Galbraith is that many of our industries – textile, furniture, buildings, clothing, advertising – survive in otherwise inhospitable surroundings because of their juxtaposition to the arts. Further, there is ample evidence that they survive better in consequence than the steel mills, coalmines and factories which are devastated by modern economic policy. The industries which survive best are those that co-exist with a strong artistic tradition.

The arts world has proved to be honourable in helping to enrich the lives of the whole nation, and indeed the world, even when finding the work of the artists exploited by every conceivable medium (television, radio, records, tape, publishing houses, video recordings, film, advertisements, newspapers and magazines) for what the Performing Rights Society has proved is wholly inadequate returns and in many cases no returns or royalties whatsoever.

The arts world has proved to be honourable simply by going on – and going on in the face of inadequate funding and often imminent bankruptcies. It has worked, over the years, within available subsidies. The bankruptcies have indeed been rare – the West of England Theatre Company in 1958 and Prospect Productions Limited in 1978 – with a few voluntary liquidations in the thirty intervening years (Carl Rosa, D'Oyly Carte, the Renaissance Theatre Company in Barrow-in-Furness and Meadow Players in Oxford).

The arts world has proved to be honourable, but can it go on being so in the face of any Government proving itself to be dishonourable? This is not a political matter. For the sake of less than £1 million the Government has risked destroying future credibility in the arts world. The next time the Arts Council intimates a level of subsidy and asks a Company to plan on this basis what is the answer to any Company asking: "Can we rely on that figure?". This is not a legal or financial question of commitment; it is a fundament question of responsibility.

Luckily, governments come and go. Civilisations are outlived, but "the arts represent the substance of faith; they are what we find again when the ruins are cleared away". (Flowering Judas – Katherine Anne Porter)

ASSETS AND ACHIEVEMENT

My Alport Lecture (page 162) was published in The Journal of Arts Policy & Management (Vol. 1, no 1 – Feb. 1984). I followed this with a paper delivered at one of the City University's Research Weekends in 1984 which was also then published in The Journal of Arts Policy & Management.

It is interesting to note that this paper refers to the Arts Council's Housing the Arts funds; this was long before the National Lottery. The important conditions of these capital funds being made available by Jennie Lee, the first Arts Minister, were that they were closely tied to the performing companies then being in receipt of annual subsidy and all future estimates and accounts for these companies should include proper depreciation reserves to ensure the reasonable maintenance of these buildings. Further, Housing the Arts funds were offered towards improving facilities in order to maximise future income; for example, the restaurant extension at Liverpool Playhouse. Lastly, the Housing the Arts funds were intended to be repaid to the Arts Council should the buildings in receipt of such funds no longer be used for the purposes intended. What price the Thorndike, Leatherhead or the Redgrave, Farnham now – and what have been their auditors' responsibilities over the ensuing years?

This paper also raises the matter of 'exploitation of product' and particularly refers to promotional activities which have grown enormously since the first days of Cats. The Disney stage production of The Lion King generates some £25,000 per performance, which is taking some £100,000 in ticket sales.

Assets and Achievement

My Alport Lecture dealt with Commitment and Responsibility. This lecture's subject passes to the opposite side of the Balance Sheet containing the Assets out of which one pays commitments.

The reason I am pursuing an analysis of Balance Sheet items is because professionally-trained arts administrators should not only be able to read a Balance Sheet and know what kings of Assets and Liabilities have to be dealt with, but also should be able to relate them to the human aspects of running an arts organisation. Depending on the size of the organisation, the arts administrators leave the detailed financial matters either to the Accountant or Finance Director, or to the Board members or Trustees, or to the Auditors.

In the Alport Lecture I attempted to show what the simple Balance Sheet item of 'Commitments' means in terms of human responsibility; responsibility from the government to the Arts Council, the Arts Council to its clients, its clients to the artists and the artists to the nation.

I now want to analyse the Assets and relate them to the achievements of an organisation and how they can and should be utilised to help the organisation and its creative artists go on to even greater achievements.

The Dictionary defines assets as funds or property available for payment of debts; the estate of an insolvent or deceased person; or the entire property of a business company; a thing of value.

Fixed assets may be regarded as those assets of a business which are of a permanent or at any rate long-term nature, and are definitely held for the purpose of earning revenue and not with a view to resale (e.g. Plant and Machinery, Buildings, etc.).

Apart from Fixed Assets, a Balance Sheet might contain Current (or Floating) Assets which are those usually held for only a short period of time, and which are expected to be converted into cash within a year of the Balance Sheet date. The best examples of Current Assets are Stocks, which are held in order to be sold at a profit in the ordinary course of business, and debtors which are mainly the result of sales (at a profit) but which are at an interim stage on the way to conversion into cash. Of course, cash itself is also a current asset.

But the point of choosing today's subject is to bring home to arts administrators the importance of remembering that assets are held *for the purpose of earning revenue*. All too often the administrator of a Gallery, a Theatre, a Concert Hall or an Opera House thinks of how to meet projected expenditure by raising income; and income from the traditional sources of the box office (ticket sales), sponsorship and patronage, local authority grants and Arts Council (i.e. central government) subsidies. I would suggest that we should use the heading 'exploitation of assets' in our Estimates and Budgets to remind us of the investment that has been made in the purchase of such assets. After all, the Arts Council's criteria for grant-aid specifically includes "the fullest practicable use of facilities ..."

What are these assets? Well, first and foremost there are the buildings. Most of the buildings used by arts organisations in Great Britain have been built or re-built since 1945 with local authority and Arts Council Housing the Arts funds. Of the 100 and more theatres housing touring productions in 1939, built by commercial companies in the earlier half of the 20th century, nearly all but a handful have been lost. Those major ones which remain should be cherished: the Palace Manchester, the Theatre Royal Newcastle, the Leeds Grand, the Hippodromes in Birmingham and Bristol, the New in Oxford and the Empire Liverpool; in Scotland, the theatres in Edinburgh, Glasgow and Aberdeen, and in Wales the New Theatre Cardiff and the Swansea Grand. There is also a second tier of such theatres and small-scale circuit. The next group is the Regional Repertory Theatres, again mainly built or re-built since the war with public funds – in Sheffield, Liverpool, Manchester, Leicester, Birmingham, Bristol, Nottingham and Coventry; a second tier in such places as Ipswich, Guildford, Leatherhead, Farnham, Colchester, Derby, Exeter, Leeds and Salisbury.

Then there are the art galleries and art centres such as the Arnolfini in Bristol, the Midland Group Gallery in Nottingham, the Museum of Modern Art in Oxford, the ICA and Riverside in London, Cannon Hill in Birmingham and South Hill Park in Bracknell. These are a different problem – often the premises are indeed fully used – but the operation is too labour intensive and the buildings can be open for too many hours for too few people. Many of these buildings, costing the country many millions of pounds to build, re-build and maintain annually (and I have not yet mentioned the new buildings on the South Bank and in the Barbican Arts Centre) are utilised for public purposes for only 24 hours a week – let us say eight performances of three hours each. No doubt many administrators will rush to the defence that increasingly theatres are opening catering facilities prior to and after performances and even at lunchtimes – exploitation which Sam Wanamaker initiated at the New Shakespeare in Liverpool and later Bernard Miles developed at the original Mermaid Theatre.

Even West End theatres have been known to enter the catering field! Arts Centres will tell us they are opening for an increasing number of hours each week and art galleries will emphasise that they are open from 10.00 a.m. to 6.00 p.m. for six days a week – alas, not when the bulk of the public want them or can go to them! But that is, perhaps, another subject. The point of this discussion is that such an essential and expensive asset as the buildings which house arts activities should be exploited to the utmost degree and Boards of Companies should regularly review this subject as an item on the agenda of their meetings.

Plant and machinery in any factory is regularly reviewed as an asset to be utilised to the full insofar as it can be revenue earning. Again, in arts buildings there should be constant vigilance as to how best to exploit these assets. Sound and lighting equipment is costly and, along with the buildings in which they are housed, should be utilised more than the 30 weeks per year, which appears to be the average these days which many companies can keep playing on available funds. Studio theatres particularly should be available to many of the small-scale, often experimental companies which instead choose to tour nearby schools, libraries, disused fire stations and breweries at much greater expense to the public purse.

In the light of the Arts Council's investment over the past thirty-five years in the development of permanent drama and the buildings to house them, it was, perhaps, surprising to read Ian Watson's wholly incorrect assertions in the October 1983 issue of Entertainment and Arts Management that "permanent companies are fast disappearing with, if not the active connivance of the Arts Council, at least its obvious lack of concern". The Arts Council and its officers have spent decades in raising Government funds to help extend the permanent repertory companies to three or four week seasons with adequate rehearsals and a better balance of old and new plays. If audiences and the exigencies of the profession have conspired to make it nigh on impossible to retain a company for more than a few months, why must it be 'the Arts Council willfully failing to nourish this creative nursery of the theatre'? The fact that West End producers are currently finding it increasingly difficult to persuade major artists to sign 'run-of-play' contracts, or indeed to sign contracts for more than three months, should also according to Mr Watson's method of apportioning blame, be laid at the Arts Council's feet because that is the body that should bear the responsibility for all the failures of the arts since 1946 and none of the successes. It is indeed deplorable that the stars who are surely needed to renew West

End plays to attract investors and playgoers now often only stay long enough to collect various awards and are then off to pastures new. The run-of-play contract is now rare in a world when theatre actors have a constant eye on films and television for their lucrative earnings.

This short review of the more intensive use of arts buildings cannot be complete without reference once again to the fact that many of us who marched down Whitehall many years ago alongside Equity, Musicians Union and NATTKE members to persuade the Government to amend the Sunday Observance bill continue to be disappointed that the workers still do not benefit from the fact that the law was indeed changed. I do not know who first coined the ridiculous phrase 'unsocial hours' since all hours are social. Ask a bus conductor or a ballet dancer, ask a reporter or a theatre manager. Just as the country now has such a mixed population that a proportion of workers can be found who wish to observe their Sabbath on any day of the week from Monday to Sunday, so the population at large expect shops to be open seven days a week from early morning to late at night. Many of us know the enrichment of life, the enormous convenience and the wealth of trade which can be experienced in most major cities of the world where one can buy a book or record at 10 o'clock at night. Certainly there is every argument for some of our theatres to open for two shows on a Saturday and two on a Sunday even if it means closing on Mondays or Tuesdays. In New York the theatres stagger their performances so that there is always a show to see, seven days a week. All this gives more employment to Union members, more convenience to playgoers, more intensive use of buildings, better exploitation of productions and more convenience of choice to everyone. I remember with particular joy a packed Sunday matinee of the all-black musical *The Wiz* on Broadway attracting an audience largely from Harlem who would never have ventured out for a fashionable Saturday evening performance. The exploitation of product is, therefore, not solely a matter of finance but of social responsibility.

Turning to social responsibility brings our thoughts to two further assets, probably the most important – the actual product of the companies (the exhibitions, operas, ballets, plays, symphonies, etc.) – and the companies themselves which might be considered the 'Goodwill'. These two assets might be considered the most marketable, the most exploitable! It is becoming increasingly important in these days of waning interest in television for companies to review the possibilities of video exploitation of product. Last April the American National Association of Broadcasters released its study of television viewing habits in the U.S.A. The data was overwhelmingly negative - a complete reversal of the positive opinions six years before. A similar research paper was prepared for I.B.A. in August 1983 the Television Audience for the Arts in Great Britain. Both studies showed audiences were, even when not declining, becoming less positive about television with a growing number feeling increasingly dissatisfied. The British study showed that for programmes where audiences were small they were enthusiastic, but the programmes which attracted larger BBC and ITV audiences usually showed, on average, a less appreciative response. Similarly the U.S. study indicated that the public rated television less important in their lives than in the mid 1970s, less entertaining and less of a technical marvel. Further, one-half of the viewers said they were watching less television than in the earlier study and these findings were evident across demographic and socio-economic groups, not just among the more affluent ones who traditionally say they watch less television and hold the medium in low regard.

Perhaps there is here a new hope for increased audiences for the live arts. The study's authors state that: "Technologies which ignore human values are the most likely to be rejected. Our study confirms that consumers shy away from services that replace 'human' communication with 'mechanical' communication. As society advances technologically, people seek counter-balancing human contact." These studies perhaps mark the end of the largest and strangest love affair with technology since Henry Ford started cranking out automobiles. With the romance gone, viewers are more critical of television programmes. Now is the time, therefore, to exploit the British theatrical product. The national companies are already into this aspect of their business and it is time that many of the regional companies formed a consortium whereby opera, dance and drama productions are better exploited. I recently saw an excellent video film about the City of Birmingham Symphony Orchestra's concert version of *Porgy and Bess* and how it came about – that is the background administrative and financial planning which went into bringing it about. I am sure that such a tape could have a wide distribution on the U.S. campus circuit. All too often, unfortunately, we have purists in our organisations who ask two questions about such exploitation:

Firstly, how much will the third party make out of it? As if it matters, so long as the original production company makes a profit! And secondly, if we once agree to such exploitation we shall have to hear all our following product solely to this end. Well, look what has happened to all those arts organisations who have, indeed, sold their birthright. No doubt being aware of the dangers is alone a guarantee not to fall into them!

Passing from Fixed Assets to Current Assets takes us to Stock. These might well include scenery, props and costumes. Many theatres have long since abandoned the activity of hiring such assets out to amateur groups. Certainly the costs of transport and packing, refurbishing and cleaning, controls and costings are all so prohibitive to make one question whether this ancillary activity is worth the time and effort. The important thing is to review the situation constantly and exercise vigilance as an administrator. There are often too many stories of 'the company down the road' which does not cannibalise sets and costumes from re-use but 'throws them out' at great cost ... the major repertory companies accuse the nationals of this deplorable waste, the small repertory companies accuse the larger ones, the amateurs accuse the smaller ones and the local tobacconist accuses the amateurs.

I have not yet touched upon the more obvious aspect of Stocks – of programmes, posters, slides, postcards, greeting cards, scripts and scores, badges and other ephemera which can sell and sell. These promotional activities are all obvious, as is the need to cost the storage space required and to assess the particular qualities required in finding the right manager and sales staff to exploit these stocks.

Of course there is always the danger of companies drifting too far down the road to exploitation – and instead of exploiting their artistic product (the assets I am dealing with in this paper) they move on to money-raising ventures that are hardly even ancillary to the main objects of the company. No wonder that arts administrators, let alone artists, are impatient with the time which might be devoted to, say, a lottery; and no wonder that often such commercial ventures fail in practice because the arts administrators feel they have lost their way and are far from the original driving commitment which led them into this mad profession. What needs to be done by every board and certainly every arts administrator is to examine and re-examine priorities. Never accept that one is so over-stretched that nothing more can be done, never relax about searching the Balance Sheet for new ways of improving the work that is to be done. It may well have taken the Arts Council many decades to go back to first principles, to examine their priorities and decide what has to be done; as good arts administrators never let your board relax in its endeavours to re-examine the assets, with particular attention to the talent inherent in the artists employed, and arrange priorities to ensure that assets are used as effectively as possible.

If the new generation of arts administrators, who have been professional trained to do this, do not include this item on the agenda of each board meeting we cannot expect the lay members of boards always to be so vigilant. Income from exploiting assets can be used to extend the range of activities an organisation wishes to undertake; a bankrupt company can do nothing.

Finally, another word about Goodwill – the Goodwill that is inherent in the arts. The arts have a commercial value and it is fundamental to ensure that those benefiting from the arts activity in an arts district should be required to contribute towards that activity. Before the Lincoln Center was built it was possible to acquire derelict property in Tenth Avenue very cheaply. Subsequent to the success of the Lincoln Center the property has risen in value astronomically. *Carnegie Hall* has achieved financial stability because 46% of its income is from sources other than box office receipts and sponsorship – it is from property which it owns. Today in North America, where arts subsidies have still not acquired the respect and built-in tradition they have in Europe, it has been established that property values rise around a catalyst. The footprints of an audience making their way to the Barbican or *Cats*, to the South Bank or *Evita* are of considerable financial value. Such names as Bristol Old Vic represent Goodwill the world over. We should use this asset to the full. And also RSC's *Nicholas Nickleby* on their stages, *Brideshead Revisited* and *Jewel in the Crown* on their televisions, *Ghandi* and *Educating Rita* on their screens, and so on … What other British industry can rival these assets and achievements? Let us remember the definition of such assets – they are 'held for the purpose of earning revenue'.

POSTSCRIPT

During nearly thirty years as the Arts Council's Finance Director I found I was in control of funds that rose from under one million pounds to several hundred million. A number of colleagues often asked how on earth one managed such vast funds over the whole UK field of theatre, music, literature, the visual arts, opera and dance. I suppose the answer is that one just plodded on – one went into the office each day and picked up the next letter which needed a response, answered the next phone call and went to the next meeting. Every day of every month of every year was endlessly fascinating. If one stepped back to look at the whole national or international arts scene one might have had a nervous breakdown but one's advice to creative artists battling the same problems as an accountant in the arts scene must surely be to just get on with it.

I am always concerned about a playwright who writes a play and spends years trying to get it produced rather than writing a second, third and fourth play and suddenly hitting the right formula. Similarly, a performer has to keep at it. Don't set one's sights on a narrow horizon because one never knows what an unexpected meeting or a different approach can produce.

Also, one has to keep reminding oneself that problems have to be broken down over time and participants. For example, the National Theatre Company was launched at the Old Vic whilst waiting for the years it took to build the three auditoria that were to house the company. In its early years under Sir Laurence Olivier productions were critically and financially successful. But suddenly, as with all theatrical ventures, the company hit a bad patch and the losses mounted. I attended a Board Meeting when the directors turned to me as they found it impossible to cope with a deficit of some £45,000. This was an horrific sum and in those days the Arts Council had no such reserve funds. It was impossible to consider the National Theatre going bankrupt before it had even taken occupation of its new building on the South Bank.

I pointed out that the problem had to be broken down, first between the participants, who were the Greater London Council (GLC), the Arts Council of Great Britain (ACGB) and the National Theatre itself (NT). Thus each might be asked to find £15,000, still an impossible sum. But then the need could be spread over, say, three years. Thus each participant should have to find £5,000, the NT's contribution coming from increased income.

The impossible problem had become manageable. Furthermore, the unique success of *Othello*, with Olivier, resulted in its transfer to the Cambridge Theatre and the three contributors of £5,000 in the first year then found that the unexpected profit of £30,000 from the transfer cleared the balance.

There is an old Persian folk tale about a thief about to be beheaded. As he was being led to the chopping block he called out to the King "If you spare my life I'll teach your horse to sing hymns". The King had a sense of humour so he spared the thief's life and gave him a year to teach his horse to sing; but if he failed at the end of the year he'd go back to the block.

So the thief began to spend all his time singing hymns to the horse. All the other criminals laughed: "You'll never be able to teach that horse to sing". But the thief just smiled and replied: "I have a year. A lot can happen in a year. Maybe the horse will die. Maybe the King will die. Maybe I'll die. And, who knows, maybe the horse will learn to sing".

So the unexpected might happen. When I qualified as a Chartered Accountant I went to work for an amazing businessman, Harold Wingate. As his Finance Director one had to look after his properties, optician shops, optical works and multifarious businesses. His great personal hobby was the Curzon cinema in Mayfair, which he created, built and ran. One day I was working at the optical factory and he telephoned me to say he had bought the Comedy Theatre and, as he knew I was a young man crazy about theatre, would I come up to head office to discuss what to do with it?

I explained to him that it was one of the London theatres I would not have considered purchasing, it being dilapidated with columns in the stalls causing bad sight lines. Nevertheless, we devised a scheme to refurbish it and to pioneer the development backstage to provide better technical facilities and dressing-room accommodation with offices above which we let commercially to American Express to help subsidise the theatre. This was the very first scheme of this type which was later to be copied in London and in New York as a means by which a theatrical site could be exploited to everyone's advantage.

It is true that Harold Wingate threatened to sack me for choosing a 'crushed rose' colour for the auditorium seating when the classic colour was crimson but we overcame our differences and the musky pink colour of seats is still in evidence.

Suddenly I was faced with being landed with running a West End theatre. Harold Wingate was roaming France and Italy so that he could pioneer the foreign film policy at the Curzon cinema, with such great films as *Bicycle Thieves* and the Marcel Pagnol trilogy (*Marius*, *Fanny* and *Caesar*).

Totally inexperienced, I ran round the provinces to find a new play which might re-open the Comedy, and decided to bring in *Morning's At Seven*, on 14th December 1955, a play produced by Anna Deere Wiman, which had been touring. This was a delightful American comedy with a lovely British cast – Peter Jones, Mona Washbourne, Margaret Vines, Marda Vanne, Frederick Piper and Charles Heslop. However, although since revived successfully on Broadway, this production did not take off. I then arranged a transfer in 1956 of *The Threepenny Opera*, from the English Stage Company at the Royal Court Theatre, which was more of a success.

Personal friends in North America then mentioned to young playwrights that I was looking for new plays, and alongside a mountain of scripts from British dramatists I started to receive ones from the United States and Canada. A Professor Robert Anderson sent me a play, *Tea and Sympathy*, which I thought would go well in London and I submitted it to the Lord Chamberlain. In those days every script for public performance has to be submitted to the censorship of the Lord Chamberlain's office. Although nowadays *Tea and Sympathy* might be considered rather mild, in those days, the 1950s and 1960s, a play about a college student who thought he might be homosexual and was taken to bed by his Professor's wife to prove he was not gay, was banned from production in public, so the script went onto my shelf.

Amongst other scripts arriving daily, an Arthur Miller sent me one entitled *A View From the Bridge*, but the Lord Chamberlain could not suggest a few simple cuts and altered words since the gay element was intrinsic to the plot, so that play was also refused a licence. The third play to suffer that way was Tennessee Williams' *Cat On a Hot Tin Roof*, and I was in despair.

All these plays had been successful on Broadway. Being controversial and frank, they examined aspects of society which the drama had not hitherto explored. However, the Lord Chamberlain did not view these plays with an indulgent eye, and considered them unsuitable for the general public.

One day I was lunching with the lady who ran the Watergate Theatre Club under the arches at Charing Cross, the late Muriel Large. She bemoaned the fact that she could not find any good new plays and I responded by explaining that I had some excellent scripts which were all banned. "Let me have them!" she cried, but I pointed out that they each was too large a production to contemplate in her tiny theatre club and the US royalties would be too expensive for her to countenance. In those days, one could run a 'private theatre club' for members only, which enabled one to produce plays without them being censored in any way, subject, of course, to police raids if anyone complained about any subversive or obscene element of the production.

Some weeks after our lunch, Muriel telephoned me with the wonderfully crazy idea whereby we might move her Watergate Theatre Club into the Comedy Theatre and produce these three plays. "You're mad" I replied, "We'll all end up in prison."

But she persisted and asked me to sort it out with our lawyers. Reluctantly I proceeded to explore the possibility, which culminated with our launching the New Watergate Club in the Comedy Theatre. Harold Wingate and I recruited theatrical luminaries onto the Board, such as Donald Albery and Hugh Beaumont and with them we also formed New Watergate Productions Ltd. We were then running a West End theatre as a club, very strictly limiting attendance to members only. One could become a member for five shillings and, after 24 hours, could purchase tickets for the member and up to three guests. Everyone thought it would not work or that we would be raided by the police but, lo and behold, it did work and soon was so successful that our membership rose to 68,000.

We launched a new club with *A View From the Bridge* on 17th October 1956, directed and designed by Peter Brook and starring Anthony Quayle, Megs Jenkins, Michael Gwynn and Mary Ure. This was followed by *Tea and Sympathy* on 25th April 1957 and, finally, *Cat On a Hot Tin Roof* with Kim Stanley, Leo McKern, Paul Massie and Bee Duffell, directed by Peter Hall with designs by Leslie Hurry. This production opened on 30th January 1958 and played on Tuesdays to Sundays at 8.30p.m. (with matinees on Wednesdays and Saturdays). We thought we had pioneered the big break through of Sunday night performances!

The New Watergate Club proved so successful we even extended into the Globe Theatre (now the Gielgud) with club members being offered seats for *The Potting Shed* by Graham Greene with Irene Worth, Gwen Frangcon Davies and John Gielgud, directed by Michael MacOwan.

Even further, the New Watergate Club presented such revues as *Share My Lettuce* with Kenneth Williams and Maggie Smith, enabling us to present sketches which could not be tampered with by the Lord Chamberlain.

Having driven a coach and horses through the theatre censorship laws we soon found that Parliament abolished the Lord Chamberlain's powers of theatre censorship. Thus, to all those students of theatre who point to me as the 'guy who got rid of theatre censorship', I can only respond that I never set out to do that. I simply wanted to produce three worthwhile American plays and the rest just followed.

The club having fulfilled its initial purpose then ceased to exist; although the New Watergate Presentations Company continued to produce in the West End.

Nowadays, seeing the insipid film version of *Tea and Sympathy*, or subsequent productions of the Tennessee Williams and Arthur Miller plays, one wonders what all the fuss was about. My one lasting memory was to have welcomed Arthur Miller to the opening night of *A View From the Bridge*, when he was accompanied by his then new wife, Marilyn Monroe.

INDEX

42nd Street 22, 127

Abercrombie, Nigel 144
Absence Of War, The 120
Act Now! 105, 106, 107
Actor's Theatre 96
Adelphi Theatre 38, 105
Adler, Luther 52
Adler, Stella 52
Affair, The 52
Afore Night Comes 110
After Mrs Rochester 51
Albee, Edward 99, 115
Albert Hall 38, 149
Albery, Donald 184
Albery, Sir Bronson 145
Albery Theatre 60, 61
Aldwych Theatre 23
All The Year Round 84
Allen, Woody 50
Almeida Theatre 59, 60, 61
Ambassador Extraordinary 84
American Express 182
American Group Theatre 52
Amy's View 60, 122
And The World Goes Round 59
Anderson, Malcolm 150
Anderson, Maxwell 52
Anderson, Robert 183
Andorra 110
Angels 27
Annie Get Your Gun 39, 131
Another Country 99
Anything Goes 122, 123
Apollo Theatre 23, 96, 106
Arden, Leslie 133
Arnold, Matthew 90
Arnolfini 174
Art 19, 25, 60, 109
Art Theatre 113
Arts Council of England 106, 143
Arts Council of Great Britain
    11, 39, 41, 47-53, 62, 65-68, 91,
    92, 96, 98, 105, 108, 110, 116,
    117, 137, 138, 141, 143-145,
    150-178, 181
Arts Theatre 96, 106
Arts Theatre, Salisbury 111
As You Like It 109, 110
Ashcroft, Dame Peggy 22, 145
Asner, Ed 95
Aspects of Love 37, 41, 128
Astaire, Fred 70
Astoria Theatre 96
Athens Concert Hall 76, 102, 103
Atkins, Eileen 99
Atkinson, Rowan 23
Attenborough, Lord Richard 155
Aukin, David 127, 128, 129
Awake and Sing 52
Ayckbourn, Sir Alan 23, 109

Bailey, Mark 148
Bailey, Pearl 22
Balanchine, George 147
Ballets Russes 147
Barbican Arts Centre 138, 149, 174
Barbican Pit 96, 109
Barbican Theatre 120, 179
Barnum 37, 39, 41
Bart, Lionel 134
Batt, Mike 147, 149
Battersea Arts Centre 59
Baudin, Martine 102
BBC
    53, 59, 95, 103, 116, 117, 141, 143,
    177
Beaton, Alistair 119
Beaumont, Binkie 116
Beaumont, Francis 90
Beaumont, Hugh 184
Beautiful Game, The 70, 71
Beecham, Thomas 113
Beggar's Opera, The 90
Belasco Theatre 83

Belgrade Theatre, Coventry 111
Bell, James 112
Bennett, Alan 17
Bennett, Michael 159, 169
Bent 129
Bernstein, Leonard 155
Berry, Eric 14
Bertram Mills Circus 151
Best of Friends, The 22
Betrayal 109
Bicycle Thieves 182
Bigger Splash, The 169
Billington, Michael 98
Billy 122
Billy Elliot 70, 71, 117
Birmingham Repertory Theatre
     11, 108, 110, 119
Birmingham Symphony Orchestra 177
Bitter Sweet 86, 122
Blithe Spirit 85
Blond, Neville 91
Bloom, Leslie 82
Bloomer Girl 40
Bond, Edward 110
Born Yesterday 95
Bragg, Melvyn (Lord) 127
Braithwaite, Lilian 82
Branagh, Kenneth 23
Breaking the Code 22
Breath of Life, The 122
Bremen, Arnold 102
Brentford Public Baths 149
Brideshead Revisited 179
Bridewell Theatre 57, 59, 60, 61
Brief Encounter 43
Briers, Richard 111
Bristol Old Vic 14, 105, 179
BRIT School 42
British Phonographic Industry 41
Britten, Benjamin 53
Broadway Theatre 93
Brook, Peter 149, 184
Brough, Colin 22
Brown, Ian 145
Browne, Wynyard 145

Bubbling Brown Sugar 40
Building Jerusalem 150
Burbage, James 89
Bury, John 145
Bush Theatre 59, 61, 148
Bygraves, Max 39
Byrne, Patsy 111

Cabaret 49, 122
Café Puccini 85, 117
Calendar Girls 118
Cambridge Theatre 70, 182
Cameron Mackintosh Visiting Professor of
     Contemporary Theatre 127
Candide 149
Cannon Hill 174
Caramitru, Ion 102
Careless Rapture 122
Carey, Joyce 43
Carl Rosa Opera Company 151, 170
Carmen Miranda Story, The 126
Carnegie Hall 179
Carousel 38, 40, 131
Casablanca 112
Cat On a Hot Tin Roof 92, 183, 184
Catastrophe 116
Cats 37, 41, 55, 85, 96, 117, 125,
     127, 147, 152, 155, 157, 169,
     172, 179
Cause Célèbre 119
Cavalcade 85
Century Theatre 131, 132
Channing, Carol 22
Charles II 87
Chekhov, Anton 123
Chelsea Palace 59, 148
Chess 127
Chichester Festival Theatre 109, 117
Chicken Soup with Barley 111
Chorus Line, A 155, 169
Citizens Theatre, Glasgow 110, 148
City University
     11, 12, 13, 40, 127, 154, 159, 160, 172
Clark, Sir Kenneth 144
Clark, Stephen 133

Closer 60
Cobb, Lee J 115
Cochran, Charles B 116, 151
Codron, Michael 98, 116
Cogo-Fawcett, Robert 105
Coliseum Theatre 43, 80, 116, 131, 148
Collins Music Hall 148
Comedy Theatre
    15, 92, 106, 119, 182, 183, 184
Company 40, 96, 129, 132
Congreve, William 90
Contemporary Dance Trust 101
Continental Divide 120
Copenhagen 17
Cottesloe, Lord 144
Cottesloe Theatre
    83, 96, 119, 120, 148, 149
Coward, Sir Noel
    19, 43, 52, 79, 85, 86, 92, 109, 122,
    145
Cowardy Custard 59
Crawford, Dan 57, 61
Crawford, Michael 37, 39, 122
Crazy Gang 23
Cressida 87
Criterion Theatre 106
Critic, The 34
Croft, Neville 84
Crosbie, Annette 110
Crucible Theatre, Sheffield 110
Cuckoos 109
Cummings, Constance 145
Curtain Theatre 89
Curzon cinema 15, 182

Daily Telegraph 13
Daldry, Stephen 117
Daly's Theatre 86
Dancing Years, The 85, 122
Dankworth, Alec 149
Dankworth, John 138, 149
Daughters Of The Revolution 120
David, Elizabeth 49
Davies, Dame Gwen Frangcon 184
Dean, Sir Basil 86

Dear Augustine 111
Dear God Thank You For The Blessings 133
Death Of A Salesman 115
Delicate Balance, A 115
Deloitte & Touche 70
Dench, Dame Judi 122
Derngate Theatre, Northampton 149
Design for Living 109
Devine, George 52, 91
Dews, Peter 145
Dewynters 148
Dillane, Stephen 82, 83
Disney 172
Doble, Frances 79
Doctor's , The 119
Doll's House, A 98
Domingo, Placido 37
Dominion Theatre 121
Donmar Warehouse 59, 61, 82, 96, 148
D'Oyly Carte 170
Dress Circle 121
Drewe, Anthony 122
Drury Lane Theatre
    53, 71, 87, 90, 95, 121, 122, 131,
    132, 148
Dry Rot 23
Duchess Theatre 132
Duffell, Bee 184
Duke of York's Theatre 22, 70, 84, 85, 86
Duncan, Ronald 91
Dyke, Greg 53

Earls Court Arena 148
Edgar, David 120
Educating Rita 155, 179
Ehle, Jennifer 82
Eliot, T.S. 21, 66, 92, 125
Elsom, John 101
Elton, Ben 70
Embassy Theatre 96, 148
Embassy Theatre, Swiss Cottage 59
EMI 53, 112
Empire, Hackney 109
Empire, Holborn 148
Empire, Kingston 96, 148

Empire, Liverpool 174
Empire, Shepherd's Bush 148
Empire, Wood Green 148
Emrys-Williams, Sir William 143, 144
English National Opera 38, 80, 116
English Stage Company
        52, 68, 91, 98, 183
Entertainer, The 52
Entertainment Managers' Association 33
Equity 34, 167, 176
Esmee Fairbairn Foundation 110
Euripides 110
Evening Standard Drama Awards 93
Everding, Professor August 103
Everitt, Anthony 144
Evita 123, 125, 127, 147, 179
Ewing, Maria 38
Eyam 133
Eyre, Charmian 111

Fantasticks, The 59, 62
Farnham Castle Theatre 14
Faure 38
Featherstone-Witty, Mark 41
Feelgood 119
Fernald, John 14
Festival Hall 38, 149
Fiddler On The Roof 70
Filer, Roger 97
Findlater, Richard 145
Finlay, Frank 111
Finsbury Park Empire 59, 148
Fire Station, Oxford 148
Five Guys Named Moe 132
Fletcher, John 90
Floyd Collins 60
Follies 39, 123, 127
Follow My Leader 119
Fonteyn, Dame Margot 37
Forbidden Broadway 59
Forbidden Planet, The 128
Ford, Henry 177
Fortune Theatre 59
Fosse 71, 115
Four Weddings and a Funeral 118

Fox, Robert 99
Fox, Robin 91, 145
Franz, Joy 95
Frayn, Michael 17
Frederica 40
Friedman, Maria 125
Friml, Rudolf 39
Fringe, The 18, 19, 96
Frisch, Max 110
Frogs, The 149
Fry, Christopher 92
Funny Girl 39
Furth, George 132

Gag Company, The 104
Galbraith, Professor 169, 170
Gallery First-Nighters
        79, 80, 82, 83, 84, 85
Gambon, Sir Michael 23, 87
Gandhi 155, 179
Gardner, Herb 22
Garfield, John 52
Garrick, David 90
Garrick Theatre 119
Gate Theatre, The 96
Gateway Players 13
Gateway Theatre 96
Gay, John 90
Gay Landscape 110
Gaylord Ravenal 38
Ghetto 123, 129
Ghosts 119
Gielgud, Sir John 22, 37, 116, 145, 184
Gielgud Theatre 60, 106, 124, 184
Gielgud, Val 145
Gilbert and Sullivan 67
Glamorous Night 85, 122
Glasgow, May 144
Globe, Bankside 87
Globe Theatre 124, 184
Glyndebourne 149
Golden Boy 52
Goldsmith, Oliver 90
Goodman, Lord 12, 66, 117, 144
Gozo 72, 74, 76

Grade, Michael 49
Grand, Leeds 174
Grand, Swansea 174
Granville Theatre, Walham Green 59, 96
Grayson, Michael 32
Greater London Arts 65
Greater London Council 181
Green, Hughie 34
Green, Simon 39
Greene, Graham 184
Guardian, The 13
Guildhall School 37, 41
Guinness, Sir Alec 22, 34
Guthrie, Tyrone 66, 145
Guys and Dolls 25, 124
Gwynn, Michael 184

Hadrian VII 59
Hahn, Dagmar 102
Half Moon Theatre 132
Hall, Sir Peter 99, 109, 184
Hallé Orchestra 11, 14, 67, 138, 150, 156
Hamlet 23
Hammerstein, Oscar 87, 89, 122, 129
Hampstead Theatre 61, 96, 119, 120
Hapgood 23
Hardwicke, Sir Cedric 84
Hare, David 119, 120, 122
Harris, Tom 101
Harvard University 12
Harvest Moon Rising 133
Harwood, Ronald 99
Hauser, Frank 145
Hawthorne, Sir Nigel 98
Haymarket Theatre 35, 106
Hayward Gallery 141, 170
He Said My Father Was A Farmer 133
Healey, Sir Dennis 166
Hedley, Philip 108, 145
Heintz, Eckhard 103
Hello Dolly 22
Henceforward 23
Her Majesty's Theatre
    23, 55, 72, 122, 124, 132
Hesketh-Harvey, Kit 133, 148, 149

Heslop, Charles 183
Heywood, John 89, 90
Hiller, Dame Wendy 22
Hilton, James 25
Hippodrome, Birmingham 174
Hippodrome, Bristol 174
Hippodrome, Golders Green 59, 148
Hippodrome, Manchester 67
His Majesty's Theatre 86
Hobson, David 133
Hockney, Sir David 159, 169
Hoffman, Dustin 51, 98, 115
Holborn Empire 148
Hollywood 35, 46, 70
Holt, Thelma 19, 98
Home Chat 86
Home, William Douglas 84
Honk! 122
Hope-Wallace, Philip 131
Horatio 133
Hoskins, Bob 124
Howard & Wyndham 108, 116
Howard, Jason 38
Hudson, Richard 148
Hunting of the Snark, The 147
Hurry, Leslie 184
Hylton, Jack 38
Hytner, Nicholas 37, 122, 153

I Married an Angel 169
Ibsen, Henrik 92, 119
ICA 174
Iceman Cometh, The 115
I'm Not Rappaport 21, 22, 23, 35, 59
Imperial Theatre, New York 131
Inspector Calls, An 120
Interpreters 99
Into The Woods 95, 123
Iphigenia 110
Irving, Sir Henry 91
Irving Theatre 96, 148
ISPA 100, 101, 102, 103, 104, 112
ITV 35, 177

Jackson, Glenda 22

Jackson, Sir Barry 108
James, Peter 145
Jenkins, Lord Hugh 145
Jenkins, Megs 184
Jennings, Alex 53
Jermyn Street Theatre 57, 59
Jerry Springer the Opera 122
Jewel in the Crown 155, 179
John Offord Publications 11
Johns, Ian 79
Johnson, Bill 131
Jones, Martin 135
Jones, Peter 183
Jonson, Ben 90
*Joseph and his Amazing Technicolour
    Dreamcoat* 127
Journey's End 119
Julius Caesar 14
Justifying War 119

Kafka's Dick 99
Kanin, Garson 95
Kathy and I Show, The 95
Kaufman, Gerald 152
Kaye, Danny 39
Keel, Howard 38
Keeling, Stephen 134
Kelly, Gene 70
Kelly, Matthew 34
Kent, Jonathan 61
Kent, Nicholas 61
Kenwright, Bill 99
Kern, Jerome 38
Kerryson, Paul 132
Kert, Larry 132
Keynes, Lord 144, 160
Killing Fields, The 155
Kind Hearts and Coronets 34
King Lear 98, 102
King's (Hammersmith) 59
King's Head, Islington 57
King's Head Theatre 59, 148
King's Rhapsody 85, 122
King's Theatre, Hammersmith 96
Kingsley, Sydney 52

Kingston Empire 59, 96, 148
Kipling, Rudyard 30
Kiss Me Kate 131
Koch, Martin 148

La Rue, Danny 22
La Scala, Milan 130
La Traviata 38
Laine, Dame Cleo 38, 149
Lambert, JW 145
Lambrakis, Christos 76
LAMDA 41
Lange, Jessica 99
Large, Muriel 183, 184
Last Night of the World, The 130
Lawrence, D H 109
Lawrence, Gertrude 34, 123
Lawrence of Arabia 22
Lean, Sir David 43
Lee, Jennie 172
Lehar, Franz 39
Leicester Haymarket 105, 169
Lend Me A Tenor 96
Lennon 96
Les Misérables
    25, 37, 41, 55, 85, 96, 117, 123, 124,
    125, 129, 133, 147
Lettice and Lovage 96, 99
Levis, Carol 34
Levy, Benn 145
Lewenstein, Oscar 52, 91, 145
Lewis, Daniel Day 23
Libertine, The 118
Library Theatre, Manchester 13
Lincoln Center, New York 179
Lion King, The 172
Little, Sir Emile 84
Littlewood, Joan 13, 155
Liverpool Playhouse 14, 172
Liverpool School For Performing Arts 159
Livings, Henry 13
Lloyd Webber, Lord Andrew
    41, 46, 70, 92, 95, 121, 152
Lock Up Your Daughters 59
London Symphony Orchestra 103, 138

Long Day's Journey Into Night, A 99
Longman, Peter 108
Look After Lulu 52
Look Back in Anger 52, 68, 91
Lord Chamberlain 90, 91, 92, 183, 184
Lord of the Rings, The 121
Lost Horizon 18, 25
Lowry Centre, Salford 109, 116
LuPone, Patti 123, 124, 125, 126
Lyceum Theatre 148, 149
Lyly, John 89
Lynch, Alfred 111
Lyric, Hammersmith 43, 51
Lyric Studio 59
Lyric Theatre 23, 35, 106

MacDonalds 47
Mackay, Fulton 110
Mackintosh, Iain 148
Mackintosh, Sir Cameron
    37, 41, 46, 47, 53, 85, 92, 105,
    106, 113, 116, 117, 122, 125, 127,
    128, 129, 130, 132, 134, 147, 159, 169
MacLeod, Alison 111
MacOwan, Michael 145, 184
Madame Butterfly 71, 130
Madhouse in Goa, A 99
Madness of George III, The 17
Majestic Theatre, New York 131
Malkovitch, John 47
Malta 72, 74, 113
Mamet, David 116
Mamma Mia! 80, 93
Manolopoulos, Nicos 102
Marathon Man 51
Marius, Fanny and Caesar 182
Marlowe, Christopher 87, 89, 90
Marriage of Figaro 38
Martin Guerre 85, 117
Martin, Mary 123
Marvin, Lee 115
Marx Brothers 112
Mary Poppins 121
Mary Rose 14
Massie, Paul 184

Massinger, Philip 90
Maxie 134
May, Val 145
Maybox 97
Mayflower Theatre, Southampton 109
Mazeppa 80
McCartney, Sir Paul 42, 113
McConnell, James 133
McCutcheon, Martine 34
McDonald, Jane 34
McKellen, Sir Ian 23, 35, 102
McKenna, Shaun 134
McKenzie, Julia 123, 124, 125, 126
McKern, Sir Leo 145, 184
McTeer, Janet 98
Me and Juliet 89, 92
Me and My Girl 96
Meadow Players, The 170
Medea 99
Melnikoff, Anthony 110
Mendes, Sam 61
Menuhin, Yehudi 37
Merchant of Venice, The 83, 98
Mercury Theatre 96
Mermaid Theatre 47, 59, 62, 98, 174
Merman, Ethel 123, 125
Merrily We Roll Along 61
Metcalfe, Carol 61
Midland Group Gallery 174
Midsummer Night's Dream, A 116, 149
Miles, Lady Josephine 144
Miles, Lord Bernard 59, 62, 144, 174
Miller, Ann 23
Miller, Arthur 110, 115, 129, 183, 185
Miller, Jonathan 84
Milne, A A 13
Minnelli, Liza 39, 123
Minogue, Dannii 34
Miranda, Carmen 126
Miss Saigon
    37, 41, 71, 113, 123, 125, 128, 129,
    130, 133
Mitchell, Julian 99
Mitchell, Yvonne 145
Moby Dick 85, 117, 147

Moliere 144
Money to Burn 121
Monroe, Marilyn 185
Montague, Helen 22
Montgomery, Marion 149
Morison, Patricia 131
Morning's At Seven 183
Most Happy Fella, The 169
Mother, The 117
Mothers Against 120
Mousetrap, The 62
Mr Cinders 59
Mr Pym Passes By 13
Mrs Warren's Profession 52, 91
Much Ado About Nothing 110
Mundy, Simon 102
Munro, George 110
Murmuring Judges 120
Murray, Braham 109
Museum of Modern Art 174
Musicians Union 176
My Fair Lady 34, 53, 72, 105, 169
Mysteries, The 148, 149

National Theatre
    49, 102, 103, 116, 119, 125, 127,
    152, 153, 154, 181
NATTKE 176
New Lindsey Theatre 96, 148
New Moon Theatre 40
New Shakespeare, Liverpool 174
New Theatre, Cardiff 174
New Theatre, Oxford 174
New Vic, Stoke on Trent 148
New Watergate Club 92, 184
New Watergate Presentations Company 185
New Watergate Productions 184
New York Met 67
Nicholas Nickleby 149, 155, 179
Nichols, Peter 134, 145
Night At The Opera, A 112
Night in Casablanca, A 112
Noble, Adrian 98
Noises Off 155
North-Whitehead, Alfred 161

Northcott Theatre, Exeter 156
Northern Arts 65
Northern Philharmonic Orchestra 38
Notre-Dame de Paris 34
Notting Hill 118
Nottingham Playhouse 110
Novello, Ivor 19, 85, 86, 92, 122
Nunn, Sir Trevor 83, 122, 155
Nunsense 59

O' Brien, Timothy 145, 147
O' Casey, Sean 144
O' Neill, Eugene 115
O' Toole, Peter 22
Odets, Clifford 52, 92
Oedipus Rex 34
Off Broadway 59, 61, 62
Oh What A Lovely War 155
Oklahoma! 40, 105, 130, 131, 169
Old Bailey 74
Old Vic 14, 35, 47, 65, 66, 181
Oldham Coliseum 132
Olivier Awards 93
Olivier, Lord Laurence
    34, 51, 52, 95, 109, 115, 145, 181,
    182
Olivier Theatre 83, 124
Olympia 148
On The Farm 133
On The Twentieth Century 124
On Your Toes 147
Opera House, Manchester 67
Opera North 37, 38, 39, 67
Orpheus Descending 98
Osborne, Charles 40
Osborne, John 52, 91
Othello 116, 182
Other Place, The 96
Out Of This World 117
Oxford University 123

Pacific Overtures 40
Pack of Lies 22
Pagnol, Marcel 182

Paige, Elaine 34
Palace Theatre 41, 124
Palace Theatre, Leicester 105
Palace Theatre, Manchester 67, 174
Palace, Walthamstow 59
Palladium Theatre 37, 96
Papp, Joseph 159, 169
Party 59
Pauli, Helmut 102
Peer Gynt 35
Peggie, Andrew 133
Pember, Ron 144
Performing Rights Society 170
Permanent Way, The 119, 120
Peters, Clarke 132
Pettersson, Allan 136
Phantom of the Opera
     23, 37, 41, 54, 55, 72, 85, 96,
     117, 122, 128, 133
Piaf 155
Piccadilly Theatre 67, 147, 156
Pick, John 11, 12, 127, 150
Pilbrow, Richard 145
Pinero, Sir Arthur Wing 91
Pinter, Harold 109, 116
Pinza, Ezio 147, 169
Piper, Frederick 183
Pivac, Jeff 102
Pizza on the Park 148
Playhouse, Liverpool 14
Playhouse Theatre 43, 57, 106, 119, 148
Plowright, Dame Joan 145
Polytechnic of Central London 12
Pompidou Centre 75
Pooley, Sir Ernest 144
Popstars 35
Porgy and Bess 177
Porter, Cole 39, 122, 131
Porter, Katherine Anne 171
Portillo, Michael 152
Potting Shed, The 184
Prince Edward Theatre 147
Prince Hal 125, 132
Prince of Wales Theatre 106
Private Lives 85

Private Prosecutor, The 111
Producers, The 121, 122
Prospect Productions Limited 170
Pryce, Jonathan
     99, 121, 123, 124, 125, 126
Ptasznski, Andre 127, 128
Public Theatre, New York 169
Pugh, David 109, 116
Pulford, Richard 100, 102, 103
Purple Rose of Cairo 50

Q Theatre 59, 96, 148
Quast, Philip 123, 124, 125
Quayle, Anthony 184
Queens Theatre 106

Racing Demon 120
RADA 14, 37, 41
Rattigan, Terence 92, 119, 120
Real Thing, The 82, 155
Really Useful Group 47
Redgrave Theatre, Farnham 172
Redgrave, Vanessa 98, 99, 117
Redington, Michael 22, 98
Refalo, Dr Michael 74
Regional Arts Board 67, 68, 146
Renaissance Theatre Company 23, 170
Requiem 38
Return To The Forbidden Planet 127
Rhys, Jean 51
Richard III 102
Richardson, Sir Ralph 35, 82, 85, 145
Richardson, Tony 52, 115
Rickman, Alan 98
Rigg, Dame Diana 99
Rigoletto 84
Riley, Barry 54
Rink, The 39
Rivera, Chita 123
Riverside Studios 57, 59
Robertson T W 91
Robinson, Sir Kenneth 144, 160
Rodgers, Richard 39, 122, 129
Romance, Romance 59
Romeo and Juliet 71

Ronnie Scott's 148
Rooney, Mickey 23
Rose 22
Roundhouse, The 148
Royal Ballet 154
Royal Ballet School 37, 73
Royal Circle 82, 85
Royal Coburg Theatre 66
Royal College of Music 37, 41
Royal Court Theatre 43,
    52, 91, 106, 110, 183
Royal Exchange, Manchester
    67, 98, 109, 110, 148
Royal Festival Hall 149
Royal Opera Company 154
Royal Opera House 43, 56, 161
Royal Shakespeare Company
    37, 38, 39, 46, 63, 96, 98, 99, 125,
    149, 154, 155, 179
Royal Victoria Hall Foundation 65
Rudkin, David 110
Run For Your Wife 96

Salad Days 105
Salisbury Playhouse 110
San Francisco Symphony Orchestra 149
Sanders, Martijn 102
Sarah, Peter 101
Saroyan, William 52
Savoy Theatre 23
Schlesinger, John 51
School for Scandal 14, 90
Schools for Performing Arts Ltd 41, 42
Scofield, Paul 21, 22, 35, 115
Scottish Arts Council 143
Scottish Opera 67
Scottish Symphony Orchestra 103
Sea, The 110
Seagull, The 99
Secret Garden, The 98
Selfridges 34
Semi-Monde 19, 98
Sex Lives Of The Potato Men 117
Shadowlands 129
Shaffer, Peter 99, 145

Shaftesbury Theatre 62, 106
Shakespeare in Love 87
Shakespeare, William
    80, 87, 89, 90, 115, 122, 123, 124,
    144
Share My Lettuce 184
Shared Experience 51
Sharp, Sir Kenneth 167
Shaw, George Bernard 52, 91, 119, 144
Shaw, Irwin 52
Shaw, Sir Roy 41, 66, 145, 164
She Stoops To Conquer 90
Sheffield University 13
Shepherd's Bush Empire 59, 148
Sherek, Henry 25, 116
Sheridan, Richard Brinsley 88, 90
Sherman, Martin 99
Shirley Valentine 96
Show Boat 37, 38, 39, 127
Side By Side With Sondheim 123
Side Man 60
Siegfried Sassoon 96
Silvester, Victor 38
Sinden, Donald 145
Singin' in the Rain 39
Single Spies 96
Sirocco 79, 86
Smetana Theatre, Prague 103
Smith, Dame Maggie 99, 184
Sneeze, The 23
Snow, C P 52
Soapstars 35
Soho Theatre 19
SOLT 28, 32
Sondheim, Stephen
    39, 61, 95, 122, 125, 127, 129,
    132, 133, 134, 144, 149
Song and Dance 147, 169
South Bank Centre 100
South Hill Park 174
South Pacific 131, 147, 169
Spacey, Kevin 47
St James Theatre, New York 131
St James's Theatre 110
St John Stevas, Lord Norman 131, 164

Stage, The
13, 25, 32, 61, 89, 110, 116, 144,
145, 147, 152
Stanley, Kim 184
Steele, Tommy 39, 41
Stephen Joseph Theatre in the Round,
Scarborough 148
Stephenson, Pamela 128
Stewart, Rod 80
Steyn, Mark 40, 123, 125, 126, 130
Stilgoe, Richard 125
Stoll-Moss 97, 108, 116
Stones in his Pockets 19, 70, 71
Stoppard, Sir Tom 144
Strand Theatre 35, 52, 96, 106
Strassen, Michael 134
Streatham Hill Theatre 59
Streetcar Named Desire, A 99
Streisand, Barbara 39, 123
Stritch, Elaine 132
Student Prince, The 40
Stuff Happens 119, 120
Styles, George 122
Styne, Jule 125
Sugar Babies 23
Sullivan, Dan 22
Sunday In The Park With George
123, 124, 125, 128, 130
Swan Theatre 96
Sweeney Todd 132

Tamburlaine the Great 89
Taming Of The Shrew, The 116
Tavistock Theatre, The 96
Tea and Sympathy 92, 183, 184, 185
Tearle, Michael 101
Tell Me On A Sunday 147
Tempest, The 87
Teuchies, Hilde 101
Theatre Investment Fund 106, 147
Theatre Projects Consultants
48, 67, 76, 103, 132, 148, 149
Theatre Royal, Bath 109
Theatre Royal, Newcastle 174
Theatre Royal, Stratford East 108, 155

Theatre's Management Association 32
Theatres Trust 105, 106, 108
There's Only One Jimmy Grimble 70, 71
This Is Going To Be The Best Day Ever 133
Thompson, Peter 148
Thorndike Theatre, Leatherhead 111, 172
Three Sisters, The 98, 115
Three Tall Women 99
Threepenny Opera 183
Tillius, Sven-Gunnar 102
Time Warner 112
Times, The 79, 106
TKTS 55, 106
Tod, Peter 32
Toms, Carl 145
Tone, Franchot 52
Tonight's The Night 80
Torch Theatre, The 96
Tosca 130
Traitor's Gate 13
Tree Grows in Brooklyn, A 40
Tricycle Theatre 59, 61, 119
Tulip Fever 118
Twelfth Night 110
Two by Two 39
Two Ronnies, The 96

Udhe, Milan 100
Uncle Vanya 23
Unity Theatre 96
Upstairs Downstairs 155
Urdang Dance Academy 72
Ure, Mary 184

Valentine, Anthony 111
Van Gyseghem, Andre 145
Vanbrugh, John 90
Vanne, Marda 183
Variations 147
Vaudeville Theatre 23, 105
Venue Theatre 121
Verdi, Guiseppe 84
Verdon, Gwen 123
Veronique 40
Victoria Palace 23

View From the Bridge, A
92, 110, 183, 184, 185
Vines, Margaret 183
Vita and Virginia 99

Waiting For Godot 99
Waiting for Lefty 52
Wallace, Neil 102
Walpole, Robert 90
Waltz Dream, A 40
Wanamaker, Sam 174
Wandsworth Prison 66, 71
War and Peace 112
Warner Brothers 112
Washbourne, Mona 183
Watergate Theatre 96, 148, 183, 184
Watford Palace 132
Watson, Ian 175
Watty, Mark 149
We Will Rock You 80
Webb, Paul 13
Webster, John 90
Weede, Robert 169
Weekend, The 35
Weir, The 60
Welcome to Canada, Jennie 133
Weldon, Duncan 98
Welsh Arts Council 143
Welsh National Opera 67
Wembley Arena 53, 147, 148
Wesker, Arnold 111
West End 19-27, 31-35, 43, 46-48, 51,
54, 56,-62, 68, 71, 72, 92, 93,
95- 97, 105-109, 124, 127, 128,
130-133, 147, 148, 151, 155,
168, 175, 182, 184, 185
West of England Theatre Company 170
West Side Story 70, 71, 129, 155, 157
West Yorkshire Playhouse 110
Wharmby, Denise 133
*When I Was a Young Girl I Used to Scream
and Shout* 96
When She Danced 99
Which Witch? 148
White Horse Inn 25

Whiting, John 145
Willatt, Sir Hugh 144
Williams, Kenneth 184
Williams, Robbie 53
Williams, Tennessee 183, 185
Williams W E 169
Wilson, Angus 52
Wilson, Josephine 144
Wilson, Julie 131
Wilson, Manning 14
Wilson, Richard 35
Wiman, Anna Deere 183
Wingate, Harold 182, 184
Wingate, Roger 97
Winslow Boy, The 119, 120
Wiseman, Thomas 111
Wit 60
Wiz, The 176
Wolfensberger, Rudolf 101
Wolsey Theatre, Ipswitch 49
Woman in Black 19, 96
Woman in White, The 121
Wood Green Empire 59, 148
World of Paul Slickey, The 38
Worth, Irene 184
Wright, Nicholas 87
Writers' Centre 19
Wycherley, William 18, 90
Wyndham, Charles 82
Wyndham's Theatre 85, 117

You Never Can Tell 119
Yusupov 133

Zorina, Vera 169

ENTERTAINMENT TECHNOLOGY PRESS

FREE SUBSCRIPTION SERVICE

Keeping Up To Date with

Pages From Stages

Entertainment Technology titles are continually up-dated, and all major changes and additions are listed in date order in the relevant dedicated area of the publisher's website. Simply go to the front page of www.etnow.com and click on the BOOKS button. From there you can locate the title and be connected through to the latest information and services related to the publication.

The authors of the title welcome comments and suggestions about the book and can be contacted by email at: af@tpcworld.net

Titles Published by Entertainment Technology Press

ABC of Theatre Jargon *Francis Reid* **£9.95**
This glossary of theatrical terminology explains the common words and phrases that are used in normal conversation between actors, directors, designers, technicians and managers.

Aluminium Structures in the Entertainment Industry *Peter Hind* **£24.95**
Aluminium Structures in the Entertainment Industry aims to educate the reader in all aspects of the design and safe usage of temporary and permanent aluminium structures specific to the entertainment industry – such as roof structures, PA towers, temporary staging, etc.

Basics - A Beginner's Guide to Stage Lighting *Peter Coleman* **£9.95**
This title does what it says: it introduces newcomers to the world of stage lighting. It will not teach the reader the art of lighting design, but will teach beginners much about the 'nuts and bolts' of stage lighting.

Basics - A Beginner's Guide to Stage Sound *Peter Coleman* **£9.95**
This title does what it says: it introduces newcomers to the world of stage sound. It will not teach the reader the art of sound design, but will teach beginners much about the 'nuts and bolts' of stage lighting.

A Comparative Study of Crowd Behaviour at Two Major Music Events *Chris Kemp, Iain Hill, Mick Upton* **£7.95**
A compilation of the findings of reports made at two major live music concerts, and in particular crowd behaviour, which is followed from ingress to egress.

The Exeter Theatre Fire *David Anderson* **£24.95**
This title is a fascinating insight into the events that led up to the disaster at the Theatre Royal, Exeter, on the night of September 5th 1887. The book details what went wrong, and the lessons that were learned from the event.

Health and Safety Aspects in the Live Music Industry *Chris Kemp, Iain Hill* **£30.00**
This title includes chapters on various safety aspects of live event production and is written by specialists in their particular areas of expertise.

Hearing the Light *Francis Reid* **£24.95**
This highly enjoyable memoir delves deeply into the theatricality of the industry. The author's almost fanatical interest in opera, his formative period as lighting designer at Glyndebourne and his experiences as a theatre administrator, writer and teacher make for a broad and unique background.

Focus on Lighting Technology *Richard Cadena* **£17.95**
This concise work unravels the mechanics behind modern performance lighting and appeals to designers and technicians alike. Packed with clear, easy-to-read diagrams, the book provides excellent explanations behind the technology of performance lighting.

An Introduction to Rigging in the Entertainment Industry *Chris Higgs* **£24.95**
This book is a practical guide to rigging techniques and practices and also thoroughly covers safety issues and discusses the implications of working within recommended guidelines and regulations.

Lighting for Roméo and Juliette *John Offord* **£26.95**
John Offord describes the making of the production from the lighting designer's viewpoint - taking the story through from the point where director Jürgen Flimm made his decision not

to use scenery or sets and simply employ the expertise of Patrick Woodroffe.

Lighting Systems for TV Studios *Nick Mobsby* **£35.00**
Lighting Systems for TV Studios is the first book written specifically on the subject and is set to become the 'standard' resource work for the sector as it covers all elements of system design – rigging, ventilation, electrical as well as the more obvious controls, dimmers and luminaires.

Lighting Techniques for Theatre-in-the-Round *Jackie Staines,* **£24.95**
Lighting Techniques for Theatre-in-the-Round is a unique reference source for those working on lighting design for theatre-in-the-round for the first time. It is the first title to be published specifically on the subject, it also provides some anecdotes and ideas for more challenging shows, and attempts to blow away some of the myths surrounding lighting in this format.

Lighting the Stage *Francis Reid* **£14.95**
Lighting the Stage discusses the human relationships involved in lighting design – both between people, and between these people and technology. The book is written from a highly personal viewpoint and its 'thinking aloud' approach is one that Francis Reid has used in his writings over the past 30 years.

Pages From Stages *Anthony Field* **£17.95**
Anthony Field explores the changing style of theatres including interior design, exterior design, ticket and seat prices, and levels of service, while questioning whether the theatre still exists as a place of entertainment for regular theatre-goers.

Practical Guide to Health and Safety in the Entertainment Industry
Marco van Beek **£14.95**
This book is designed to provide a practical approach to Health and Safety within the Live Entertainment and Event industry. It gives industry-pertinent examples, and seeks to break down the myths surrounding Health and Safety.

Production Management *Joe Aveline* **£17.95**
Joe Aveline's book is an in-depth guide to the role of the Production Manager, and includes real-life practical examples and 'Aveline's Fables' – anecdotes of his experiences with real messages behind them.

Rigging for Entertainment: Regulations and Practice *Chris Higgs* **£19.95**
Continuing where he left off with his highly successful *An Introduction to Rigging in the Entertainment Industry*, Chris Higgs' new book covers the regulations and use of equipment in greater detail.

Sixty Years of Light Work *Fred Bentham* **£26.95**
This title is an autobiography of one of the great names behind the development of modern stage lighting equipment and techniques.

Sound for the Stage *Patrick Finelli* **£24.95**
Patrick Finelli's thorough manual covering all aspects of live and recorded sound for performance is a complete training course for anyone interested in working in the field of stage sound, and is a must for any student of sound.

Stage Lighting for Theatre Designers *Nigel Morgan* **£17.95**
An updated second edition of this popular book for students of theatre design outlining all the techniques of stage lighting design.

Technical Marketing Techniques *David Brooks, Andy Collier, Steve Norman* **£24.95**
Technical Marketing is a novel concept, recently defined and elaborated by the authors of this book, with business-to-business companies competing in fast developing technical product sectors.

Theatre Engineering and Stage Machinery *Toshiro Ogawa* **£30.00**
Theatre Engineering and Stage Machinery is a unique reference work covering every aspect of theatrical machinery and stage technology in global terms.

Theatre Lighting in the Age of Gas *Terence Rees* **£24.95**
Entertainment Technology Press is delighted to be republishing this valuable historic work previously produced by the Society for Theatre Research in 1978. *Theatre Lighting in the Age of Gas* investigates the technological and artistic achievements of theatre lighting engineers from the 1700s to the late Victorian period.

Walt Disney Concert Hall *Patricia MacKay & Richard Pilbrow* **£28.95**
Spanning the 16-year history of the design and construction of the Walt Disney Concert Hall, this book provides a fresh and detailed, behind the scenes story of the design and technology from a variety of viewpoints. This is the first book to reveal the "process" of the design of a concert hall.

Model National Standard Conditions *ABTT/DSA/LGLA* **£20.00**
These *Model National Standard Conditions* covers operational matters and complement *The Technical Standards for Places of Entertainment*, which describes the physical requirements for building and maintaining entertainment premises.

Technical Standards for Places of Entertainment *ABTT/DSA* **£30.00**
Technical Standards for Places of Entertainment details the necessary physical standards required for entertainment venues.